the Idler

ISSUE 36 | WINTER 2005

First published in Great Britain in 2005

10 9 8 7 6 5 4 3 2 1

The Idler, Issue 36

First published by Ebury Press, Random House, 20 Vauxhall Bridge Road, London SW1V 2SA

Random House Australia (Pty) Limited
20 Alfred Street, Milsons Point, Sydney, New South Wales 2061, Australia
Random House New Zealand Limited
18 Poland Road, Glenfield, Auckland 10, New Zealand
Random House South Africa (Pty) Limited
Endulini, 5A Jubilee Road, Parktown 2193, South Africa
The Random House Group Limited Reg. No. 954009
www.randomhouse.co.uk
A CIP catalogue record for this book is available from the British Library.

Cover illustration by Bill Sanderson
Text design and typesetting by Gavin Pretor-Pinney

ISBN 0091905133

Papers used by Ebury Press are natural, recyclable products made from wood grown in sustainable forests.

Printed and bound in Germany by Appl, Wemding

WHAT IS THE IDLER?

The Idler is a magazine that celebrates freedom, fun and the fine art of doing nothing.

We believe that idleness is unjustly criticized in modern society when it is, in fact, a vital component of a happy life.

We want to comfort and inspire you with uplifting philosophy, satire and reflection, as well as giving practical information to help in the quest for the idle life.

THE MUTOID WASTE COMPANY 78

CONTENTS

THE IDLER
Issue 36, Winter 2005

CONTENTS

THE IDLER
Issue 36, Winter 2005

EDITOR'S LETTER

It's a strange fact, as Edward Chancellor proves in this issue, that Money doesn't exist. My debt depends on someone else credit, and vice versa. Money is just a vast global balancing act. The injection of money and capital into societies inevitably causes more problems than it solves. Which is why today's money-worshippers such as Geldof, Curtis and Bono are barking up the wrong tree when they say they want to make poverty history. It is not poverty that is the problem; peasant cultures have lower levels of stress and higher levels of freedom and fun than hard-work, rich cultures. No, wealth is the problem and the only effective campaign would be Make Wealth History. Anyway, I am just beginning to realise that money is the problem, not the solution. Take, for example, CRASS. Penny Rimbaud and his gang of disaffected dreamers live the lives of kings in their Essex cottage and acre of land. All day free to do as they please in the most beautiful surroundings, and this has been achieved on a budget of nought pounds. Penny writes powerfully on the money ethic in this issue.

Money is presented to us as the answer, the supplier of freedom, when it is itself the enslaver. In Medieval times, a healthy disrespect for money and for making money for its own sake was preached by the Catholic Church. To be poor was to be holy; the poor were not looked down upon and pitied, they were rather venerated. In fact, there seemed to be an ongoing competition between saints as to who could live the poorest. Some saints lived in holes and never washed and survived on wild berries. It was in Medieval times that the Guild system of working came in. Guilds of stonemasons, carpenters and the like set themselves up with sophisticated codes of conduct based on the values of mutual aid and fairness rather then competition. Read Arthur J Penty's revealing article for an insight into a more humane age.

We also have interviews with *Flashman* creator George Macdonald Fraser and with Corinne Maier, author of *Hello Laziness*, the international best-seller which advocates slacking off in the workplace as a means of retaining one's dignity while keeping the paycheck. On a practical note, we've also got pieces on how to travel for free (hitchhiking) and how to live for free (squatting). You don't actually need money to live like a king and even, in the words of DH Lawrence, to create your own little aristocracy, a paradise on this earth.

Tom Hodgkinson
Tom@idler.co.uk

IDLER CONTRIBUTORS

Who are the Idlers?

Aaron Burtch spends his days fishing, working landscaping jobs for cash and rehabilitating his exquisitely injured shoulders, as well as fucking about in a band called Grandaddy.
Graham Burnett is an anarchic gardener and runs spiralseed.co.uk
Simon Busch is a freelance journalist
Adam Buxton is the comic genius who was part of Adam and Joe and is now filming his own films
Edward Chancellor is the author of *Devil Take The Hindmost: A History of Financial Speculation* (Macmillan)
Andy Council's artwork can be seen at www.farmyardeez.com
Matthew De Abaitua is always available
Brian Dean runs the excellent website anxietyculture.com
Nicky Squidbunny Deeley once came home and her house was filled with bees, she now lives at www.squidbunny.net
Chris Donald is a chubby, balding ex-Viz editor, author, pile sufferer and bad tempered father-of-three
Chris Draper is an illustrator antiquarian and beekeeper
Bill Drummond is a serial father
Hannah Dyson draws anthropomorphic creatures and other beings
Nathan Fletcher is an illustrator based in Bristol. See more of his work at www.mybrokenshoe.com
Andy Franks is hoping to be free
Jay Griffiths is the author of Pip Pip: A Sideways Look At Time (Flamingo)
Paul Hamilton regrets nothing, not the divorce, the bankruptcy, the homelessness or the prison record. He would do it all again, except sit through Love Actually
Jeff Harrison is a painter, illustrator and misanthropist from east London
Joe Harrison is a comical, talented all-round good guy. Need we say more?
Anthony Haythornthwaite is an illustrator for hire, to contact him email anthony@aqhthestudio.co.uk
Eva-Kajsa Hedstrom is an illustrator who likes hot weather and meeting people. She can be contacted at evakajsasbigtrain_78@hotmail.com
Shane Hegarty works for the *Irish Times*
Damien Hirst is an artist
Stewart Home's webiste is stewarthomesociety.org
Aaron Howdle is an animator, graphic designer and illustrator who loves robots. His work can be seen at www.aaronhowdle.co.uk
Tony Husband is an award winning cartoonist who works for the *Times*, the *Express*, the *Sun*, *Private Eye* and many many more. He also performs a live cartoon poetry interactive stage show with Ian Macmillan. For more information visit tonyhusband.co.uk
Anne-Celine Jaeger is a freelance journalist
Fanny Johnstone writes about sex and cars in the *Daily Telegraph*
Dan Kieran edited *Crap Towns*, *Crap Jobs* and *Crap Holidays*. His next book is out in October 2006
Chloe King is an illustrator. She can be reached at chloeking@f2s.com
Rowley Leigh is head chef at Kensington Place, food writer for the *FT* and author of No Place Like Home. He also led the Idler team to their historic *University Challenge* victory over the *Financial Times*

IAN VINCE

HANNAH DYSON

NICKY DEELEY

NICHOLAS LEZARD is a critic and does the Slack Dad column in the *Guardian*
MARK MANNING is sometimes Zodiac Mindwarp
AIMEE MCLACHLAN lives and works from home in South London, has cat and garden for distractions. Website: aimeemclachlan.co.uk
ANDRZEJ LIGUZ is a photographer, whose work can be seen and bought at www.moreimages.net
PETE LOVEDAY is a jobbing artist, self-buried in Devon. He created the legendary Russell comics. Find out more at ccnewz.com
EDWIN MARNEY is an illustrator who generally works for dull business magazines. Visit his website at edwinmarney.co.uk
BEN MOOR is an actor, comedian and lovely man
KEVIN PARR is a writer and angler. He can sometimes be found on the A33 near Winchester
DANIEL PEMBERTON is far too successful for his own good
RACHEL POULTON is a mother and photographer
PENNY RIMBAUD is a philosopher
JOHN RIORDAN thinks Western culture peaked with Motown. You can see his drawings at www.johnriordan.co.uk
GREG ROWLAND is a legitimate businessman
BILL SANDERSON has been a full-time illustrator for 25 years. His work can be seen at www.billsandersonart.com
GWYN VAUGHN ROBERTS lives in Wales and can only produce work when his mental state is a fine balance of energy and misery
IAN VINCE is a left-handed, Mac-compatible, asthmatic comedy writer, clearly looking for some kind of niche market. He runs socialscrutiny.org
WALSHWORKS illustrations can be found at www.eastwing.co.uk and www.walshworks. org.uk
GED WELLS is Insane. See him at www.insane.org.uk
CHRIS WATSON has a new t-shirt label at

JAY GRIFFITHS

www.tonuppress.com and his work can be seen at www.chris-watson.co.uk
TONY WHITE is the Idler's Literary Editor. He's just co-edited (with Matt Thorne and Borivoj Radakovic) a new fiction anthology called *Croation Nights*, which is published by Serpent's Tail
ANDY WORTHINGTON is the author of *Stonehenge: Celebration and Subversion* (Alternative Albion)
CHRIS YATES is a legendary fisherman, photographer, master of idleness and author of *The Secret Carp* (Merlin Unwin)
WILL YATES is a fifteen-year-old illustrator with a bright future ahead of him.

NOTES FROM THE COUCH

JEFF HARRISON

THE IDLER'S DIARY

WE HELD a splendid readers' weekend in the grounds of Dial House, the cottage and garden where members of CRASS and their associates have been living together for forty years. Camp Idle brought together twelve readers with *Idler* Editor Tom, John Nicholson, John Moore and Jay Griffiths, author of *Pip Pip: A Sideways Look at Time*. The sun beat down as we wandered through the gardens, lay in hammocks and talked about the important things. We ate cake, drank champagne and listened to Noel Coward playing on the Dansette. We ate good food. On the Saturday night, John Moore played his songs and we sat round the campfire till late. The weekend was a great success and we plan to make it an annual event. Sign up on the website to be informed of future Camp Idles and other relevant events.

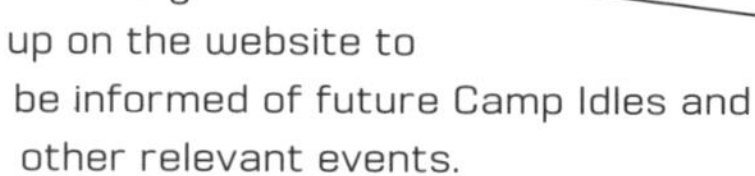

WORK ON our new book *Crap Holidays* is now complete and the book is published around now. It's terrifically funny as well as being an indictment of the awfulness of tourism and the whole idea of holidays. Surely it's cheaper and more fun simply to stay at home? Johnny Rotten sang, "I don't want a holiday in the sun," and JG Ballard has also attacked the idea that somewhere you can "find

TOM HODGKINSON JABBERS ON AT CAMP IDLE, ABOVE, AND JOHN MOORE IGNORES HIM (RIGHT). PICS BY CECILIA NICHOLSON

yourself" by going abroad. Also it has to be said that fifty weeks of hell and two weeks in paradise is not a great deal.

TOM HODGKINSON'S book *How To Be Idle* was published in the US and acclaimed as "a literary gem... irresistable" by *USA Today* and excerpted in the *New York Times*. It was even up there in the US Amazon bestsellers list, albeit briefly, alongside titles such as *Coach: Lessons on the Game of Life*. The paperback is available here with extra material.

OUR CREATIVE DIRECTOR, Gavin Pretor-Pinney, launched The Cloud Appreciation Society earlier in the year. It argues that the clouds are Nature's poetry and fights against the banality of blue-sky thinking, whereever it is found. Members receive a certificate and a badge for little more than the cost of postage. We are pleased to report that there are now 1,400 members in twelve countries around the world and the society's website (www.cloudappreciationsociety.org) received seven million hits last month. This means that Gavin has had to do a lot of envelope stuffing, but it also suggests that his book, *The Cloudspotter's Guide* (published by Sceptre), is set to be an international bestseller when it is out in the spring of next year.

OUR TEA CORRESPONDENT, Chris Yates, had a little impromptu fishing match recently, pitting his battered fifty-year-old rod and reel against the seventeen foot, ultra-light carbon match rod and hi-tech tackle of famous specimen hunter Martin "fearsome" Bowler.

Fishing together at a pond for the rare and elusive crucian carp, Martin caught a very creditable eleven, while our correspondent netted an astonishing thirty-one. Asked afterwards how he'd done it, our man confessed it was all down to the tea. Throughout the long day

ABOVE: CLOUD APPRECATION SOCIETY MEMBERS BADGE, LEFT: CUMULUS CLOUDS SHAPED LIKE A PAIR OF CATS DANCING THE SALSA BY MIKE RUBIN, MEMBER NO.329

"A WAY OF LIFE IS ON TRIAL TONIGHT"

Martin had only drunk coffee from a flask while our correspondent consumed countless pots of tea made freshly on the bank-side with his low-tech Kelly kettle. Unfortunately for "fearsome" the whole event was being covered for a feature in the *Angling Times*.

"A WAY OF LIFE IS ON TRIAL TONIGHT," said *Idler* Sports Editor John Moore as the *Idler* team took their places on University Challenge. For those of you who missed this momentous event in idling history, the Idler was pitched against a team from the *Financial Times* and we totally whipped their sorry arses, mainly thanks to team member Rowley Leigh, who answered about 90% of the questions. The show was broadcast in July and represented one of our best ever pro-idleness propaganda campaigns, coming as it did right at the heart of the beast of the establishment. It was recorded in Manchester and we took the town that night, and also had a very enjoyable drink with question master Jeremy Paxman, a charming man and a big fan of *Idler* Tea Correspondent and champion angler Chris Yates.

READERS' LETTERS

DEAR IDLERS,

I read *How To Be Idle* while lying in bed both during the mornings and the evenings; while lolling in my hammock; before taking a nap while at work; while drinking a bottle of vintage Port and smoking a cigar and being naked (thereby combining elements of Chapters 6pm, 8pm and 1am); during and after lunch; while watching the river behind my home slide by (*sans* pole and bait); while listening to classical music through a set of headphones; and on numerous walks with my cat, an excellent rambler. Finally, vindication!

Six Pack Jack Ward

DEAR IDLERS,

It's now a case of what we can do together to alleviate or cure this mass stagnation of the human spirit. No wonder whole generations go awry (disaffected youth etc), and the politicians thinking remain (at present) on their traditional wavelengths, so the radical solution required will never be. Come the Revolution! Who knows?

Thanks for an illuminating read, the historical perspective, along with all the humour added in made for an uplifting read. The websites listed at the back of the book, are potentialy a tour de force, in effecting change in one's life

Gary (Derbyshire)

GOOD AFTERNOON/EVENING, CHAPS,

I'll assume it's not the morning that you're reading this mail, and with good reason I imagine. Anyway... thought you might enjoy this little lark I had today. About a month ago I went for an interview for a bank job. Usually nothing could cause me to stir from my gentle canter through life but an efficient and coersive girlfriend has persuaded me to head off to New Zealand for a bit, so I need the kablingi. Interview over and succcessfully negotiated all I had to do was wait for the call up. The job itself was ideal, with the shifts only running in the afternoons, leaving me to work in my usual occupation in a sleepy college library of an evening.

However, all was not well. I found out about four days ago that my easy going job would be preceeded, somewhat awkwardly for a man of my laid back nature, by a three week training course. Which was running from nine to five every day. Which would be work. Which I was not in the business of enjoying.

This morning I went into the bank for the first time. At nine. Maybe I hadn't had enough sleep. Maybe I wasn't in the mood. Maybe it was because late last night I had started reading How To Be Idle.

But what I did was out of character to say the least. When no-one was looking I stood up and walked out. I walked calmly out of the building and even more calmly out of the job. 25 minutes into my banking career I had accomplished a tremendous feat.

My spirits were dampened a tad when I recieved an irate phone call from a woman claiming that they had been worrying that I had had an accident on the premises and that was the reason for my disappearance. I hung up let the sun of freedom shine on me.

My girlfriend will kill when she discovers my sloth but I will defend myself well. You need not to fear for me.

Keep up the good work

Anon

Write to us at: **The Idler**, Studio 20, 24-28A
Hatton Wall, London EC1N 8JH or tom@idler.co.uk

DEAR IDLERS,

I have not been an enthusiastic part of the modern workplace since 1973 when I bid farewell to a promising career as a solicitor. Since that time I have sailed, renovated and built large yachts, studied etching and printmaking in Jerusalem, established a vineyard and winery near Sydney and then gone on to be a printmaker, also in Sydney, www.jletching.com.au. In all these activities I have had the great good fortune to be modestly successful, certainly enough to keep going and avoid accountability to others.

Remarkably during this period I have never felt that I have actually been at work, even when much has been achieved there has always been the sneaking suspicion that something is being got away with. For thirty one years I have religiously followed your prescriptions re, sleeping in, further naps, sufficient alcohol, reading, conversation day dreaming etc. There is no question such an approach works.

However the sad fact is that in 2005, as for most of the time alluded to, one has to more or less conceal how pleasant life is lived this way. Most people in the mainstream can become quite resentful if you behave anything other than always busy, focused and relentlessly on message etc... to coin a phrase or two.

I suspect it must be very much more difficult to commence a productively idle life than it was in the 60s & 70s. We lived with massive social upheaval, the Vietnam War, (a big deal in Australia) a haze of dope and booze and a political and commercial system less well organized to catch you slipping out the side door. Many of my contempories are successful or otherwise subscribers to the Idler philosophy. I am not seeing replacements taking up the way of life. As far as I can determine most of generations X & Y want to be merchant bankers, own iPods, vote right wing and travel to the useful dinner party conversation list of expensive destinations.

Government and advertising propaganda are so pervasive that there will probably be fewer and fewer outside the working world created by the Industrial Revolution. I hope I am wrong. In the meantime I think I will go and open a bottle of fizz.

James Luxton

DEAR IDLERS,

Now, what about the doctors, nurses, firemen, the publishers of *Heat* magazine, etc—namely, those that which society has come to rely upon? Would it not be pandemonium if, say, the top surgeons in the country all decided to pull a few sickies a month themselves? I for one would be most irate and anxious if my (parents') house in Putney were to be set alight and to discover that most of the firefighters in my area had gone on a rugby tour to New Zealand or something. God only knows what would happen if Richard and Judy did not turn up to work, but I imagine chaos and tragedy would ensue...

Katie Rachel Grant

PS: Very well done to you and your team for your astounding performance on University Challenge! You totally thrashed the FT!!

Which just goes to show: idling pays. As for those doctors and firemen, they'll still be there, but they'll do three hour shifts and three day weeks.

SKIVERS AND

HEROES AND VILLAINS OF THE IDLE UNIVERSE

HIP FLASKS

Inspired by the sight of a gent in yachting linens stumbling around Soho in the late afternoon clutching a gin and tonic, we doff our cap to the little drink that planes a rough day smooth. This guy had a big red face with a sweep of blonde hair, which bobbed around the crowd like a buttered ham. We liked his lightly sozzled style.

COCKAIGNE

Cockaigne or Cockayne is a word from medieval legend that means an imaginary land of luxury and idleness, derived from the word for small cake (of which the houses in the imaginary land are built). It is a land in which grilled geese fly into your mouth and roasted pigs wander around with knives in their backs to make carving easier. We're still looking for it on Google Earth.

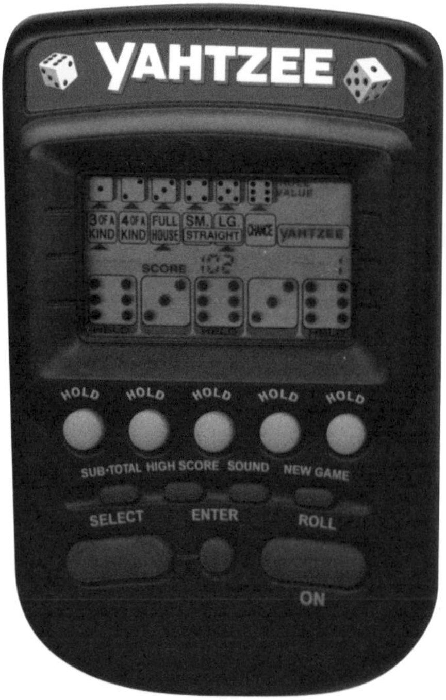

GOOGLE EARTH

Google have mapped the entire world from satellite and turned it into a 3d map that you can take little virtual trips on. Once you have tired of zooming into your own back garden, you fly low over the Sahara or sneak around the hills of the Ring Of Kerry in Ireland. Has all the joy of flying, with none of the inconvenience of the cavity searches.

YAHTZEE (left)

Now, normally we don't much like digitally-based products, they're expensive, they don't work and generally cause a lot of headache. Having said that, there's a new electronic version of the classic dice game Yahtzee which will help you while away many happy hours.

SLOW BICYCLES

Instead of forking out £300 on a snazzy bike on which you then steam round town wearing stupid neon clothes and pretending to be a courier, wobbling at the lights and shouting at taxis, buy an old no-gear bike for thirty quid, tuck your trousers into your socks and set off at a sedate pace through town, waiting at lights, tipping your hat and letting other people go first. You will arrive at your destination feeling calm, relaxed and distinctly unsweaty.

STRIVERS

TAGGING WORKERS

Tesco, Sainsbury's, Asda, Boots and Marks & Spencer are all taking advantage of satellite and radio-based computer technology to track their worker's movements, and even order them around. Removing the human initiative from warehouse work only makes the jobs even more dispiriting. Thank the Lord we spent our adolescence boning up on the dark dystopias of 2000AD, as only that comic has truly prepared us for the shiteness of the 21st century.

IPODS

The problem with all this new-fangled digital technology is that you can't fix it. Our schooling in mechanics began with the changing of needles of record players, the replacing of belts, the cleaning and aligning of tape heads. Now you drop one of these buggers and it has to be sent across the world to be repaired.

THE BBC

Now we're normally first in line to stand up for workers' rights so it must be some terrible character flaw on our behalf that we've laughing our asses off at the redundancies at the BBC. As the bourgeois gravy train crashes off the rails, those job-for-life mediocrities will have to crawl out of their endless meetings and, for a change, pull their fingers from the collective arse. By firing tranches of the buggers, the odds of us having to sit through some underling gobbling on about how their managerial notion of impartiality amounts to more than fuck all in this world are thankfully lengthening.

LONDON OLYMPICS (above badge courtesy of the Colony Room)

The worst disaster to hit London since the Millennium Dome. The smugfest in London on the day that the decision was announced was quite sick-making. The Olympics means welcoming a ton of Nazi narcissists into the city and creating a thousand godawful jobs and hideous buildings. The whole thing is colossal vanity and a waste of money and we predict big problems.

ALAN SUGAR

This loathsome slave turned master, our version of Donald Trump, is a hero to the *Daily Mail* reader. His TV show *The Apprentice* held up being a complete arsehole and wanting to make a shedload of cash as positive values.

THE TV

When your five-year-old son comes into the room and says, "Daddy, what's car insurance? Churchill do it," then you know it's time to throw the fucking thing out of the window.

THE FINE LINE BETWEEN

SMOKING & WANKING

WALSHWORKS

THE FINE LINE

Smoking	Wanking
Hate the smell of it in your hair	Ditto
Must consider feelings of others when you do it	Ditto
Hard to quit	Ditto
Can affect sexual performance	Ditto
Gives your hands something to do	Ditto
Meal in restaurant spoilt by other diners doing it all night	Ditto
A nice way to meet strangers	Ditto
Management prefer you to do it outside	Ditto
Just the sight of it excites cravings	Ditto
Twenty a day	Not any more

MDA

TONY HUSBAND'S JOKES PAGE

KNOWN TO HIS FRIENDS AS THE WORLD'S WORST JOKE TELLER, **TONY HUSBAND** ASKS A FEW FAMOUS FACES FOR THEIR FAVOURITE GAGS.

DAVID MELLOR:
An aide goes to see George W Bush.
Aide: Mr President, we need to do something about malaria.
The President pauses for a moment and replies: Give the Malarians a warning: sort yourselves out or we'll invade.

RICKY HATTON:
Quasimodo goes into a pub. He asks for a whiskey. The barman replies: "What about the bells?"

Mind your own bloody business, snaps Quasi.

DAN MCMILLAN:
Q: What did the "0" say to the "8"?
A: Like your belt.

PETE TURNER (ELBOW):
Two prostitutes talking. One says:
"Have you ever been picked up by the fuzz?"
The second one replies "No but I've been swung around by the tits."
Deric Longden - Writer
A little balloon tries to get in bed with his mummy and daddy balloon. His daddy tells him there's no room and to go to his own bed. He does but later that night he tries to sneak back into their bed but there's no room. So he lets some air out of himself. At last he can squeeze between them and he falls asleep. Next morning they awake and his dad is furious to find him there. "I'm really annoyed with you," he said. "You've let me down, you've let your mum down but most importantly you've let yourself down."

MARK RADCLIFFE:
Two cannibals are eating a clown. One turns to the other and says "Does this taste funny to you?"
And... a woman walks into a bar and asks the barman for a double entendre—so the barman gives her one.

JOHN MOORE:
David Beckham's talking to a journalist. "I think they're great. They taste great and keep your breath fresh for hours."

Posh pops her head around the door.

"Er, David, he asked you about tactics."

TONY HUSBAND:
An older man cannot sexually satisfy his young wife so he goes to the doctor. He explains that he's tried everything but he cannot satisfy her. The doctor recommends he hires a very fit handsome young bloke and gets him to hold a towel over them as they make love. The old guy hires a very attractive young guy who waves a towel over them as they make love. Again his wife is not satisfied. She suggests the young man makes love to her while her husband holds the towel. So the young man makes love to his wife while he holds the towel over them. His wife begins to orgasm. After half an hour she's exhausted and begs the guy to stop. As he stands up the old guy throws the towel at the young man and says, "*That's* how you wave a fuckin' towel, sonny."

OFF THE RAILS

Chris Donald sits back and gets extremely stressed out when he ends up travelling First Class on a Virgin train

In the olden days, when people wore top hats, the advantages of travelling First Class were obvious. At sea, for example, First Class passengers were given preferential use of the lifeboats in the event of the ship sinking. And on trains, First Class carriages had a roof. You paid extra for a First Class ticket, but you received a tangible benefit in return.

Nowadays, on Britain's trains the distinctions between First and Standard accommodation are far less pronounced. The First Class seats might be dark blue, for example, as opposed to red in Standard. In First there'll be slightly more room for your elbows, and you'll get a free newspaper, a cup of coffee and a complimentary biscuit. But you could buy a Saver ticket, a large family size selection tin of biscuits, a copy of every newspaper in WHSmiths, and fill a giant flask with coffee from Starbucks, and you'd still have a couple of hundred quid left over from the price of a First Class ticket. It doesn't add up. And yet whenever I travel long distances by train, a strange, instinctive desire to 'treat myself' always overrides the logic, and I end up paying the extra.

George Best is the same. He was once asked which of life's luxuries he couldn't do without. His reply was First Class travel. (Presumably alcohol isn't a luxury in his book.)

My wife and I recently caught a train to Oxford from our home in Northumberland. It was a five hour journey, so I decided we'd push the boat out and go First Class. I wandered into the booking office at our local station, Alnmouth, and asked for two First Class returns to Oxford. The booking clerk's eyebrows lifted dramatically when the price came up on his screen, and he asked a colleague to check that he hadn't made a mistake. Then he broke the bad news.

"I have to tell you", he said in a sombre voice, like a judge about to pass sentence, "that would be £341". That didn't seem too bad...

"Each", he added. "£682 altogether".

There were audible intakes of breath from the other passengers behind me in the queue. The alternative, I was told, would be two Saver Return tickets, at £107 each. Which did I want?

I did the sums in my head. £682, or £214. In other words, we'd be paying a premium of £472 for the luxury of First Class travel. Say, six cups of coffee between us. A couple of newspapers. Two

CHRIS DRAPER

biscuits. And the blue seat covers. Although I was desperate to find some justification for paying the extra, I simply couldn't. How could anyone justify spending £472 on an extra couple of inches elbow room on a train, when people in Africa are starving?

Then I remembered. I needed to use my laptop en route, so I would definitely need the extra space. Besides which, my mobile phone battery was flat. If I went First Class I could charge it on the train, as First Class carriages are fitted with power points beneath the tables.

I think my decision was also influenced by a book I'd been reading about the history of rail travel. It recalled how in Victorian times an order was issued to station masters advising that 'professional swimmers engaged at music halls to give demonstrations of swimming in tanks fixed upon a stage' were to be charged the same special rate of carriage as theatrical parties, plus an extra one penny per mile if their water tanks necessitated the addition of a special vehicle at the rear of the train. A similar order stated that 'monkeys accompanying an organ grinder are to be charged the same fare as dogs'. This conjured a mental image of a Standard Class carriage full of theatrical types in swimming costumes, dogs, monkeys and organ grinders.

"I'll go for First", I said, to the astonishment of the booking clerk, my wife and the passengers behind me. I was a little short of change, so I paid good for nothing

FREE

London Lifestyle Magazine.

www.goodfornothingmag.com

the £682 by credit card. Then I sat down in the waiting room feeling slightly stunned, and began to contemplate the morally indefensible decision I'd just made. The girl in the queue behind me paid £7 for a return ticket to Newcastle. A well dressed man behind her asked for a First Class return to Durham. 'At last here's someone else with a bit of class who doesn't mind spending their money', I thought to myself.

"£17", said the clerk.

I was on my own. The other passengers whispered among themselves, and looked at me as if I was a Nazi. By the time the train arrived, forty minutes late already, I was completely overcome with an awful feeling of guilt and stupidity.

It was a new Virgin train, going direct to Oxford. As we walked through the Standard carriages there was a noticeable absence of theatrical swimming troupes, monkeys and organ grinders. Just plenty of spare and comfortable looking seats, with spacious tables. And beneath each Standard class table there were two power points.

By the time I slumped down into my blue First Class seat I was feeling physically sick. I now had five and a half hours to sit and think of all the other things I could have spent £472 on.

"You've done it now", said my wife, "so you might as well just sit back and enjoy it". I tried to. Then the drinks trolley arrived.

"Would you like orange juice or still water?" asked the attendant, with a smile. "I'm afraid there's no tea or coffee today. The hot water's off".

And so began the most uncomfortable train journey of my life. I couldn't relax. I couldn't sit back and enjoy the view. How could I, knowing that in Standard Class the view was exactly the same? Instead I sat in silence, analysing and reanalysing my decision to pay the extra. I knew I'd never be at ease with myself again unless I could somehow come to terms with what I'd done.

Eventually, around about Sheffield, I broke my silence. "Look at it this way", I said to my wife. "It's not really as expensive as it seems. You see, as a higher rate tax payer, it's only really costing me sixty per cent of the £472 extra that I paid. In real terms that's only £283.20. And looking at it positively, if, when I die, I leave £283.20 in my will, then it's money that I didn't need anyway. So it will actually have cost me nothing".

BY THE TIME I STUMBLED INTO MY BLUE FIRST CLASS SEAT I WAS FEELING PHYSICALLY SICK

My wife wasn't listening, but I took considerable comfort from this philosophical conclusion. I even started to enjoy the view a little after that. And providing when I die I leave at least £283.20 in my will, travelling First Class will have been worth it.

HOW TO GET MADE REDUNDANT

Want to quit your job but need a pay-off? Andy Franks has some tips. Illustration by Nathan Fletcher

It might not be the ultimate answer, but a spot of redundancy could be just what you're looking for. A generous payout could buy you a much-needed sabbatical from the modern world, an opportunity to nourish your soul and heal your wounds before returning to the miseries of work. With careful budgeting, a decent redundancy could give you months of idling. It may even give you the time and money you need to escape properly.

So how do you do it? Well, getting made redundant is something of an art, and great cunning is needed. It's no good hanging around for years, fantasizing that your company will go down the tubes or get bought out by a multinational. You need to be pro-active about things. But it can be done, and enough of us have now been through it for there to be some valuable best practice that urgently needs to be shared among the idler community:

1. BE DEPRESSED

Depression is an illness and you can't be sacked for being ill. At the same time, depressives tend to be unproductive and have a depressing effect on those around them, so it's unlikely that anyone will want you around. It all puts you in a strong position to negotiate a nice payout. And, as an added benefit, you will almost certainly be telling the truth. But make sure you're not so depressed you just fade away from the office like a ghost, because ghosts with no money tend to be depressed and rattle their chains for a very long time.

2. BE INCOMPETENT

Enormous care is needed here: there are two obvious dangers. A spectacular act of gross incompetence will get you the sack: instant dismissal with no payout, no reference and a frantic search for another, possibly even more

arduous job. Not incompetent enough and before long you'll be getting promoted, with loads of extra hours and responsibility and even the prospect of a career. Nightmare. The key is to look like you're trying but hopelessly out of your depth.

3. GO EARLY

The great lesson from the dot.com era is that you have to take your chances. Many a hapless fool dodged the early rounds of redundancy in the mistaken belief that greater riches lay ahead. While former colleagues loafed around the globe for six months, they worked themselves to death, only to be told that the company was bankrupt, and to walk away with nothing more than the petty cash and some stationery, which they'd been habitually stealing anyway.

4. GO LEGAL

Litigation culture gets a bad press, but it's actually one of the better things to have been imported from America in recent years. Happily, it's becoming increasingly acceptable to sue your employer. If a colleague has ever made fun of your accent, raised their voice or, better still, pinched your bum, then you may have hit the jackpot. The key here is threaten to sue. Nobody, least of all you, wants to go through the effort and expense of actually taking someone to court. A lot of bluster, some legalese and nasty letters and, before long, you could be sitting down to agree an excessively generous redundancy package.

5. GO CORPORATE

Sadly, no one ever got a great payout after working in a Cornish basket weaving co-operative. The big redundancy packages go to those who spend their time fretting over spreadsheets and making the world a less interesting place. For the more pragmatic idler, you may have to undergo a year or two of this to get the deal of your dreams. It's only in the corporate world that such improbable delights as "gardening leave" exist, in which you are paid a salary only on the condition that you don't actually work, a bit like French farmers. Choose a sector particularly prone to downswings in the business cycle, be good, make yourself at home for a while, and then hit them with all of the above and more. Remember, once you've come out the other side, you may never have to go back.

CHOOSE A SECTOR PARTICULARLY PRONE TO DOWNSWINGS IN THE BUSINESS CYCLE

Then again, all that might sound like a lot of effort. Remembering that wealth is the sum of everything you value and not just things that can be measured with money (repeating this over and over as you shuffle in your pocket for some change for the bus sometimes helps), you might be better off just resigning. If your job is warping your soul that much, the Cornish basket weaving co-operative might not be such a bad idea.

WHO ARTED?

Adam Buxton is Kevin Goitre

INTRODUCTION BY TIM LOUCHE

If you're a regular viewer of Touch Me 183, the art and touching channel (between the Avago channel and the Black Entertainment Network), you'll already be familiar with Kevin Goitre. He writes and presents Nart, arguably the last serious art and culture programme in a television landscape dominated by friv and wiffle. His book *Talking Nart* and the accompanying, much bigger book, *Understanding Talking Nart* have sold well over 300 copies, many bought by people who had never even met Kevin Goitre before the signing.

Goitre was also responsible for setting up the Anthea Turner Prize to encourage the efforts of artists who once enjoyed mass acceptance only to be unfairly marginalized following a series of poor choices in their personal lives. The TV coverage of the event famously caused a stir in 2002 when Geoff Binns, the drummer from indie group Pegleg, interrupted his speech with the words, "I've got itchy balls". Touch Me 183 was inundated with six calls from an angry viewer and the ceremony was never taped as live again.

Who Arted? is the first in a series of specially commissioned features for the *Idler* which serve as an introduction to the key players of the Modern, Proto Modern, Terry Modern and Semi Bent art scene. This month Who Arted? focuses on the unfluential Semi Bent cadre of West Coast Pre Pippilists.

WHO WERE THE PRE PIPPILISTS?

Once I was in a fruit shop in the West village and then I went to a gallery to meet three people who were taking me around. When we came out there was a chat and some standing and someone said we were near where the walking scenes in *Saturday Night Fever* were shot. I started laughing and then the other people started laughing and it was like a laughing party. Then the laughing stopped very suddenly or maybe it went on for a while and petered out but to try to keep the laughing party going I said, "So Tony Manero was walking near here!" The most important of the people said, "Listen Kevin Goitre, Tony Manero ain't real! He's just John Travolta dressed up like a disco king. You fucking blow dolphins you English queer-bag." Then the laughing party broke up.

OK, so what does that have to do with Pre Pippilism? Well, maybe nothing and that's what is freaking your mind.

LITTLESAM FUCKWEST

You know that painting? The one with a man eating his hands while a pig shits on a boy dressed as a lamp? That's Littlesam Fuckwest, the Californian Pre Pippilist who caused a stir back in the late 1970s with his "anti-paintings". I should tell you the names of some of them, but I can't remember any. But anti painting

Going underground: Critic Kevin Goitre talks nart

doesn't necessarily equal anti art... or does it? Some people don't think Littlesam was a Pre Pippilist at all. Others think he was. I think he not. Was.

Yesterday I was standing in Fuckwest's studio in downtown Manhattan and he was too. "It's a rare disease these days. I was first diagnosed as a young boy," he confesses, unprovoked. "If I don't get art every hour, on the hour, I puke. Then, if I can't get to art quickly I pass out, then die."

In case you hadn't guessed yet, Fuckwest eats art. Needs to. He once tried to go without art for a

I FORGET TO MAKE THE QUESTION TURN INTO SOUND WITH MY MOUTH

whole day but by 5 O'clock his brain was so malnourished he resorted to tearing up postcards of the Impressionists and eating them with bad wine to wash the tastelessness away. "Disgusting Impressionists," spits Fuckwest with withering contempt. "Why disgusting Impressionists?" I ask him but forget to make the question turn into sound with my mouth. He doesn't reply.
Fuckwest was the best artist of the 1970s. Then he was bad for eight months in 1982. Then good again for five years. Now I don't have an opinion of him at all. I'm told he's bad.

LANE PILLOUGH

Huge name in the explosion of Bellicose Pre Pippilism. Anti Pebblism. Forgotten now. Taught fish to stop. Wrote articles about Leslie Judd. Said she was wrongly overshadowed by the more obvious dynamism of Purves and Noakes. Denied suggestions that she was not writing about artists. Maintained Judd was art. Or not art. It was good that Judd was not art. Not bad. Nad. Went back to washing her filthy pants in the 1980s.

ANDY CATPEE

(see also: Gitbus)
Abandoned Pippilism and donned a band. A band donned... you see? The band was Gitbus. They had a minor hit with "I Don't Call This Gay". Then Lelluge. You remember it. "I wish you would, I wish you would, I wish you would, swim back up the pipe. Back up the pipe! Back up the pipe! Lelluge!" You remember it.
Conversation with artist and close friend, Yollo House about Andy Catpee
Me: Why did he stop?
Yollo: Why did he stop?
Me: Is it an answer or an imitation?
Yollo: Well, I don't know. Uh, I dough-no. I'd owe no...
Me: Did he stop?
Yollo: Could we have a light on?
Me: You don't want to or you won't?
Yollo: You don't want to and I won't.
Me: More?
Yollo: He stopped.

BERG BENCHBERG CRYING

Berg Benchberg was crying. "Pippilism isn't saying anything to Greeks!" he moaned.

Andy Catpee and Yollo House were there. They told me. It was 11am. Berg was always crying they said. He cried at Sundays, empty seats, cold toast, faint praise and stains. He also cried at not saying anything to Greeks. "Why should non-Greeks get all the said?" he said when I spoke to him. He more said, "it's like something that isn't good, it's... er," bad? I ventured. "Yeah, bad," he then said.

THE LEGACY OF PRE PIPPILISM

I had something written down about the legacy of Pre Pippilism but it was written on my face and I was forced to wash it off by Kate Moss who I'm due to be dating when she's finished with the junky from the Libertines. Basically the gist of it was "none".

Next time in Who Arted? The Pre Post-Its.

CRAP JOBS: STILTON PACKER

A minibus picked me up at 5 a.m. and I clambered on amidst the huddled masses, all whey-faced and sullen. No-one spoke much for the hour-long journey deep into the still-dark countryside. On arrival, we had to change into wellies and hairnets, white overalls covering our civvies. Cunningly, the management had made sure the clocking-in machine was the other side of the changing room, so donning this uniform was a waste of your own time. Hence my wellies being a size too small, so desperate was I to get them on and get earning. Entering the dairy was a shock to the olfactory glands. To replicate this effect, leave some milk in direct sunlight for two weeks. Scoop off the resultant gloopy scum and force your face into it, snorting deeply. I looked around at my fellow workers, unable to comprehend why they were failing to react with the disgust I did. Before I could bolt, I was taken to my part of the production line. The dairy was producing a huge order of gift-set stilton and port for a supermarket chain, the cheese encased in brown ceramic pots. My job was to scoop the cheese into these pots, then seal them with wax. For twelve hours.

I tried to apply a zen-like attitude to the horrific monotony, but my co-workers failed to let my brain surf by regaling me with tales of how many temps get sacked for nicking the mini bottles of port and getting drunk in the toilets, and if we were caught eating the stilton we would also find ourselves sans employment. How anyone could eat the stilton after spending the whole day breathing it in, was beyond me.

A few hours in I started to carve little patterns into the wax seals to stop my brain from bleeding. After realising they weren't being checked these swirls and shapes became the classic cock-and balls motif, and then random sloganeering, mostly my thoughts on cheese, my opinion of the purchaser of the cheese, and, in one potentially incriminating pot, my full phone number beside the word "HELP". This made the process tolerable, but when the whistle went at 6pm I was out of my wellies and on the bus without pause, and the fresh, cheese-free air was sweet to taste.

MATT GOOLD

THE TRUTH ABOUT:

HOUSEHOLD DEBT

by Brian Dean

Average household debt in the UK is approximately £7,600, and rising. That's excluding mortgages. Contrary to press reports, it's not all about rampant consumer greed...

.....

20% OF PEOPLE use loans and credit to survive until pay-day, according to Credit Action.

24% OF PEOPLE go into debt to cover basic living costs, according to a YouGov survey.

ONE IN FIVE HOUSEHOLDS are in debt to water companies, according to the National Consumer Council (NCC).

ONE IN SEVEN HOUSEHOLDS can't afford their energy bills. (NCC)

ONE IN TWENTY HOUSEHOLDS have had their phone cut off. (NCC)

THOSE STRUGGLING WITH DEBT typically earn less than £9,500 a year, according to MORI

THE CURRENT RISE in debt hasn't been accompanied by a consumption boom, according to the Bank of England Quarterly Bulletin.

PERSONAL DEBT has grown twice as fast as income since 1997. On average, personal debt has increased by 50%, while incomes have risen by 23%.

.....

The rise in debt can be seen against a background of appallingly low incomes. In real terms (ie allowing for inflation) the bottom 10% of jobs pay less now than in 1970. The minimum wage would have to be around £6.50 per hour to bring low-pay up to the 1970 level. Meanwhile, people receiving Jobseekers Allowance must survive on only £56.20 a week.

.....

DEBT STATISTICS

BRITAIN'S PERSONAL DEBT is increasing by £1 million every four minutes.

AVERAGE CONSUMER BORROWING via credit cards, retail finance deals, overdrafts and unsecured personal loans has risen to an average of over £4,000 per UK adult—an increase of 45% since 2000.

AVERAGE HOUSEHOLD DEBT (excluding mortgages) rose from £6,800 to £7,600 over the past year.

TOTAL UK PERSONAL DEBT (including mortgages) is over £1 trillion—equivalent to a debt of £18,200 for every man, woman and child.

.....

DEBT MISERY

IT TAKES AN AVERAGE EARNER 40 DAYS to pay off the £2,400 interest on the average level of credit card and loan debt. February 10 (the 41st day of 2005) has been dubbed "Debt Freedom Day".

15% OF PEOPLE say their debts are spiralling out of control or keeping them awake at night, according to a YouGov survey.

CITIZENS ADVICE BUREAU ADVISORS have dealt with a 47% increase in personal debt problems over the last five years.

A QUARTER of those in debt are receiving treatment for stress, depression and anxiety from their GP, according to the Citizens Advice Bureau.

1.4 MILLION CUSTOMERS on electricity or gas pre-payment meters have disconnected themselves for fear of running up debt.

BANKRUPTCIES INCREASED BY 30% last year, and by

AIMEE MACLACHLAN

nearly 30% the previous year, according to the DTI.
THE BIGGEST CAUSE OF ROWS within a relationship is not infidelity but money, according to Relate.
THE AMOUNT OF DEBT being chased by bailiffs has soared by 70% over the past two years.
SAINSBURY'S BANK predicts that 30% of personal loans taken out this year will be for "debt consolidation" (ie paying off outstanding debts).

.....

The widespread financial desperation indicated above shouldn't obscure the fact that national wealth is increasing—GDP has doubled since the early 1970s. You might ask where all the wealth is going. Which leads us to the next section...

.....

BANK RIP-OFFS

Banks and credit companies see household debt as an "opportunity". Huge profits can be made from ripping off the financially desperate. Here are some typical rip-off scenarios:

LATE PAYMENT FEES

If you pay your credit card bill late, you'll automatically be charged a fee of around £20. Credit card companies make £400 million a year from such charges, according to the Consumer Association. The Office of Fair Trading believes this breaches consumer law (which stipulates that penalty charges must reflect only the bank costs incurred). But it's difficult to prove, as banks are secretive about how charges are calculated."

According to a front-page *Times* report on credit card rip-offs (27/10/04), the banks' willingness to waive card penalty fees as a "goodwill gesture" and their failure to prosecute people who refuse to pay the charges are evidence that the fees are unjustifiable. *The Times* quotes a legal expert: "Credit card penalty charges are legally unenforceable because they seek to punish the borrower rather than compensate the bank for any losses that they have suffered."

OTHER BANK CHARGES

Unauthorised overdraft fees, returned cheque fees, unpaid standing order fees, various "administration" fees, etc. *Which?* magazine found that one in four people exceeded their overdraft limit in the past year. It claims this is "a real moneyspinner for the banks". The average "mortgage arrangement fee" now stands at around £500—nearly double what it was five years ago.

CREDIT CARD CHEQUES

Some credit card companies mail these specifically to customers experiencing financial difficulty. Can't pay your water bill? Why not use our cheques? They look like normal cheques—seemingly harmless, except for the high interest rate revealed in the small print. A Consumer Association survey found that the higher a customer's debt, the more likely they are to be sent credit card cheques.

FALSE ADVERTISING

According to the Office of Fair Trading, one in five credit card advertisements breaks the law. The breaches mostly relate to misleading claims about interest rates.

SUB-PRIME LENDING

One in five people are denied access to mainstream credit and have to borrow in the more expensive "sub-prime" market, at rates that average 177%. This is "loan shark" territory, but it's a lucrative enough market (worth an estimated £16 billion a year) to attract big corporations.

PAYMENT PROTECTION INSURANCE (PPI)

This is insurance which supposedly covers customers unable to keep up credit card repayments, etc—it's generally taken up by the most financially vulnerable people. Banks use PPI as a "cash cow", with huge profit margins which are not transparent to customers. For example, the *Guardian* claimed that 10% of Barclays' worldwide profits have come from selling PPI.

.....

The *Guardian* also alleged that Barclays sponsored a secretive public relations operation called "Protect" to rebut claims of excessive profiteering on PPI. In an article entitled "Barclays exposed over huge insurance rip-off", the newspaper quotes the reaction of Norman Lamb (MP and Treasury select committee member) to its PPI findings: "It is gross profiteering, absolutely excessive, and deserves to be exposed. People need to be aware of this rip-off".

Brian Dean runs www.anxietyculture.com

(Sources, respectively: creditaction.org.uk; YouGov/KPMG survey, quoted by Press Association, 2 Sept 2003; National Consumer Council report, Sept 2003; MORI survey, quoted by *Money Observer*, 2 June 2005; Bank of England Quarterly Bulletin, Autumn 2004; creditaction.org.uk; *Guardian*, 14 Jun 2002; IFA promotion; YouGov/KPMG survey, as above; Fuel Poverty Task Force, June 2001; creditaction.org.uk; Consumer Association estimate quoted by *Daily Mirror*, 17 Oct 2003; *The Times*, 27 Oct 2004; *Which?* magazine quoted by the *Guardian*, 23 Oct 2004; OFT report, March 2004; Datamonitor, UK Non-standard and sub-prime lending 2004; *Guardian* investigation on PPI, 6 March 2004)

IDLE PLEASURES:

TREASURE HUNTS

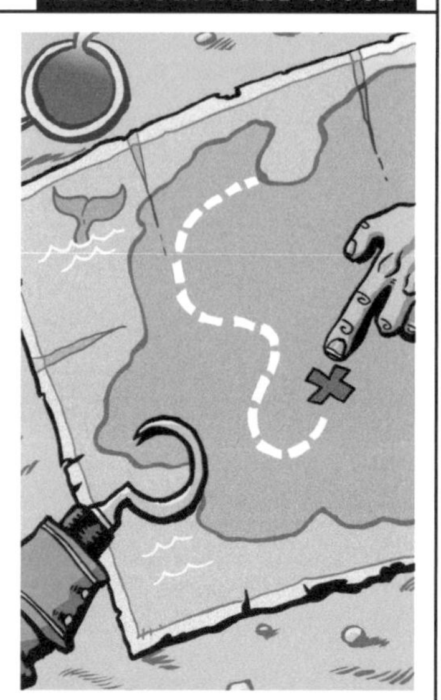

JOHN RIORDAN

The small patch of grass that passes for my back garden is now a realm of adventure. The shrubs and climbing frame morph before my eyes into an azure coastline sprinkled with palm trees. The pirate captain has buried his treasure somewhere yonder, leaving me the task of unearthing his gold. The wild dog sniffs and seeks me out, growling in defiance of my quest, but I outwit his cunning and tie him to a tree. Behind it an "X" made from bones lies in the grass. I dig, with my cutlass, and there is the chest, its hinges creak open, I'm blinded by the light, I shade my eyes, but what treasure is this? **DAN KIERAN**

CRAP HOLIDAYS:

SALTCOATS, SCOTLAND

The ugliest place to go on holiday in the UK is a small seaside town called Saltcoats. It has a caravan park that's nestled between an abattoir, full of distressed baying cows awaiting slaughter, and a chemical chimney, spewing sulphurous smoke over bottom of the range static caravans. Walk into town in the morning and you'll pass the creatures all lined up ready for the slaughter and then, on your return from the bustling metropolis that is Saltcoats, you can view the bones being conveyed into a large bin at the other end of the factory. Throw in an overexposed beach where one can view the manoeuvres of Britain's nuclear submarine fleet without binoculars and a bunch of locals sitting in sheds selling whelks in vinegar on the pier and you only get part of the grim picture.

The final insult is the weather. The relentless, battering rain colours everything—the sky, the air, the ground and the buildings. Consequently the entire place has morphed into a melancholic shade of suicidal rainwater grey. **HEATHER**

THE CLOUD APPRECIATION SOCIETY

WE BELIEVE that clouds are unjustly maligned and that life would be immeasurably poorer without them

...

We pledge to fight 'blue-sky thinking' whereever we find it. Life would be dull if we had to look up at monotonous blue day after day.

...

The clouds are Nature's poetry. We acknowledge that they are also the most egalitarian of her displays, since everyone has an equally fantastic view of them

...

We fear that clouds are so everyday as to be in danger of being overlooked. And so we seek to remind people that they are expressions of the atmosphere's moods that can be read like those of a person's countenance.

...

We believe that clouds are for dreamers, and their contemplation benefits the soul. They are the Rorschach images of the sky, and if you consider the shapes you see in them you will save on psychoanalysis bills

...

So we say to all who'll listen:
Look up, marvel at the ephemeral beauty, and live life with your head in the clouds

UK membership for just £2.00 from:
WWW.CLOUDAPPRECIATIONSOCIETY.ORG

SINGLE PARENT DAD
DAD WHY WAS I BORN
OH FUCKING HELL
GWYN

MY STRUGGLE

DAY 1 - SLOW

THE WIT AND WISDOM OF:

RICHARD PRYOR

Paul Hamilton with some of the noted comedian's best gags and quips

DRUGS

Since I stopped doing drugs I found out there's more people doing drugs—I mean, doctors'n'shit, old ladies. They call it an epidemic now: that means white folks are doing it.

I started snorting in little tiny pinches, saying, "can't get hooked, not on no coke, you can't get hooked. My friends have been snorting for 15 years—they ain't hooked."

DEATH

I want to die like my father. My father died fucking. He was 57, woman was 18. He came and went at the same time. Didn't nobody cry at his funeral. Everybody say, "Lucky motherfucker." And nobody else would fuck the woman for two years either: "No, I don't want none of that pussy, thank you, no."

Lotta people don't want funerals no more, man: "Oh no, just want flowers." I want people at my funeral when I die. Gonna pay some bitches to cry at my funeral. I want

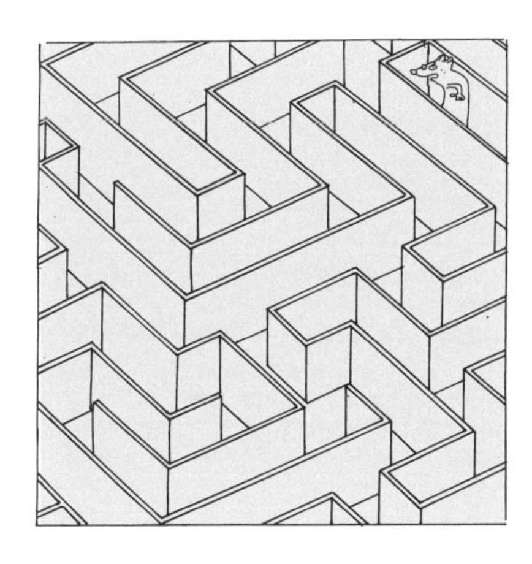

"CHINESE HAD GUNPOWDER 20,000 YEARS BEFORE A MOTHERFUCKER EVER THOUGHT OF A BULLET"

hollering'n'shit–"WAAAAH! JESUS, TECK ME WITH HIM, TECK ME WITH HIM!" And niggers take pictures at the funerals: "Now, wait a minute, git over by the casket, boy. Hold yo' momma's head up–that's good! Goddamn flash cube's done broke..." I wanna be cremated, right? Sprinkle my ashes on about two pounds of cocaine. Snort me up! Niggers be sitting around crying, "Nigger sure make a hell of a cut," (sniffs).

....

I wouldn't like to go to Heaven. Can you imagine being in Heaven, playing a harp? Sitting on a cloud, eight billion motherfuckers practicing? Dingalingaling –that's a terrible sound. (Taps microphone like a conductor's baton.) "Now, gentlemen, from the top. You three million angels in the back, lay out." Everybody in Hell be listening to Miles'n'shit.

MONEY

Since I been in showbusiness and I got some money I bought myself a house–and them motherfuckers, boy, they can kill you. Everything be 500 dollars when they come to your house. They say, "Whaddaya want? It's 500 dollars." I say, "I ain't told you what I want–" 'I don't give a fuck, it's 500.'

JESUS

You go to white church, they be quiet about Jesus. I mean, they religious, but they're quiet about their religion... See, they killed their God. When that

DAY 12- MAYBE IM TOO GOAL ORIENTATED

DAY 14- WANK

GWYN

motherfucker showed up on a donkey they hanged his ass up where they could watch him. Our God's hiding. He cool, Jack. He pretending to be a janitor.

....

(As a wino:) "Yeah, nigger, I know Jesus. I remember when the boy got killed. That's for real, man. That was on a Friday down at the railroad depot. I tried to warn the nigger. I said, 'Boy, don't you go down there fucking with them Jews without no money.'"

WOMEN

....

Bitch was so fine I wanted to suck her daddy's dick.

....

That bullshit [about] the prisoner's wife—none of 'em fuck while they was [in prison] for eight years. I wouldn't want a bitch who sit around for eight years and don't fuck. Would you? I mean, that's some sad pussy. I figure four days is enough for any woman.

WINOS

....

Winos are every place. If you name a place, say, "When the Hindenberg—" (Raucous wino voice) "I WAS THERE! Shit, I know the boy who was smoking the cigarette that made the ship burn up!"

....

Winos never get afraid of nothing but running out of wine. That's the only thing that could panic a wino. A wino could deal with Dracula: "Heyyyyy man! Say, nigger! You wid da cape! Whatcha doin' peekin' in them people's window? What's your name, bwoy? Dracula? What kinda name is that for a nigger? Where you from, fool? Transylvania? I KNOW WHERE IT IS, NIGGER! You ain't the smartest motherfucker in the world, y'know... even though you is the ugliest. Why don'tcha get your teeth fixed, nigger? That shit all hanging out your mouth... You gotta be home before the sun come up? You ain't lyin', motherfucker! See your ass in the day, you gonna get arrested... You wanna suck some blood? Get down to the blood bank, nigger. Hope you get sickle cell."

....

(Wino:) "I know how to deal with [the white man]. That's right. That's why I'm in the position I'm in today."

IT'S A WHITE, WHITE, WHITE, WHITE WORLD

....

There ain't no way to get an ambulance in the ghetto unless you call up— "There's five niggers killing a white woman!" (Screech of brakes.)

....

White people are weird. Use gunpowder. Chinese had gunpowder 20,000 years before a motherfucker ever thought of a bullet. White people had it a year and said, "We can make some bullets, we can kill people. I don't know what the Chinese are fucking off for but we can actually do damage with this shit. Motherfuck spiritual, we're after material."

Men and women fight a lot. White women 'n' white men seldom ever have fist fights. They be intellectually hurting each other—so they say. White woman says funny shit to a man: "Your dick is short and you can't even screw." White dude go (meek and defeated:) "We'll discuss it tomorrow." You say that shit to a nigger, you got a fight.

GENERALLY THE TRICKLE-DOWN
ECONOMIC MODEL HAS SERVED US
ALL RATHER WELL HERE IN
NORTH DEVON
PETE LOVEDAY

CRAP JOBS: SEWERMAN

Is there any job shittier than that of a sewerman? I'd seen the job advertised in a local rag: "manual council posts offered for gravediggers and sewermen." In essence, a straight choice between shoveling earth or shoveling shit. I opted for the softer of the two substances.

On my first day I was kitted up in the council store: helmet, donkey jacket, sewer jacket, and sewer boots. The fetching thigh-length rubber boots had hobnailed soles to prevent slippages on the limescaled bricks. Soon I was treated to one of many sewer stories. There was one about old codger Wilf who used to sit on a board wedged between the sewer walls to eat his sandwiches.

WORKING FOR THE RAT RACE

Every sewerman has a rat story. Ray, on one of his first descents, had failed to open his legs when a rat ran straight at him, causing it to run up his boots in panic. Glen was cornered by a hissing pregnant rat in a sewer side-entrance. It took me several trips into Hades before I saw my first rat, scuttling along the camber of a sewer to avoid getting its claws wet in the stream of detritus running along the bottom.

Apart from the rodents, every shit-shoveller is asked what they've seen down a sewer. My bog-standard reply would be "peanuts, tomato skin and knotted condoms"—which wasn't a lie. I did once see a goldfish flash past my boots, obviously having suffered the pet fish's equivalent of a sailor's burial at sea—the toilet flush.

Smell is the sense that most associate with a sewer. Saturdays have a distinct stench: bleach, detergent and often a sewer half full with bubbles, the start of the weekend being laundry day for much of the population at street level. In the more slower-moving low-gradient sewers, there would be a build-up of detritus and hence a strong smell of the brown stuff.

Of course, it is another world down there, walking anonymously below the public at street level, the banging of manhole covers as vehicles pass overhead, listening to the footsteps and conversations of pedestrians. Being down a sewer in London's Ironmonger Row is not most people's idea of old Victoriana, but that's exactly what it is. Under the direction of the Chief Engineer of London's Metropolitan Board of Works, Joseph Bazalgette, the Capital's network of intercepting sewers was built in the 1860s following the great stink of 1858.

Chris Hull

YOUR MONEY AND YOUR LIFE

About your name

Your name.

1.1

You can usually find your name on letters addressed to you.

Please enter your name again.

1.2

We ask for your name twice in order to fool you into revealing your true identity.

About you, the subject of our far-reaching investigations

Your identity.

1.3

Please provide evidence of your identity, existence, id and superego by providing 5 (six) recent utility bills, a sworn affidavit from an Anglican Bishop and a Statement of Personal Philosophy countersigned by a published academic specialising in the field of hive mentality.

Your Ordnance Survey Tax Reference.

1.4

The Ordnance Survey Tax Reference is a series of alphanumeric characters that enables us to pinpoint your location in Britain to within 37 centimetres, or the distance from the exact centre of your accountant to the boundary of his or her aura of honesty, whichever is the smaller.

Your position in society

If you earned less than £20,000 during the previous tax year, please fill in the rest of this form and send it to your local tax office enclosing a handwritten apology explaining why you are not contributing more to military expenditure or overtly oppressive 'security' measures.

If you earned more, or are a director of a medium to large business, ask about the tax office's 'Make it all go away with a sizeable political donation' scheme.

Roaming Genocide Miltary Dress Allowance
Tick box 1.5 if you are the leader of a regime registered with the Export Credit Guarantee Scheme and use military uniform in the dispensation of your principal duties of destroying outlying villages using arms that are manufactured in the United Kingdom.

1.5

Targetted Reliefs
Tick box 1.6 if you are a member of the Axis of Evil. Our Collateral Correspondence Section will write to you about this. You should be in to accept the delivery, which may be a heavy package.

1.6

About your charitable donations

Gift Aid
Tick box 2.1 if you would like the Ministry of Defence to claim tax relief on your donations to buy the latest weapons of mass annihilation.

2.1 [ ] The Ministry of Defence is a Registered Charity which exists to provide kudos and social skills training for educationally subnormal politicians.

About your bank

Your Bank
A bank is an institution that affects surprise when you ask it for some of your money.

2.2 [ ]

Your Business Bank Manager
Your Business Bank Manager is a young adult authorised to issue advice and 9-hole specialist ring-binders after attending an exhaustive seminar at an Essex Travelodge.

2.3 [ ]

About our make-believe world of numbers

Enter your total income from professional narcotics production in box 2.4. You can calculate this by counting the aluminium suitcases in your attic and multiplying by £25,000.

2.4 [ ]

Enter your Kidnapped Racehorse Allowance in box 2.5. Please see the Indolent Revenue leaflet *"5h3Rg4r - About Your Tax-Efficient Donations to the IRA"*.

2.5 [ ]

Enter your current electricity meter reading in box 2.6. We need to know this in order to distract you while we sort through your refuse sacks for evidence of fiscal misdemeanours.

2.6 [ ]

Declaration

I agree that
We may request and share financial and personal information from banks, employers and carelessly-selected faceless bureaucrats. I deeply respect the work of the Indolent Revenue and submit to your infinite wisdom and expertise, So Tax Me God. Amen.

2.7 [ ]

I USED TO DO NOTHING BUT TALK SHIT ALL DAY

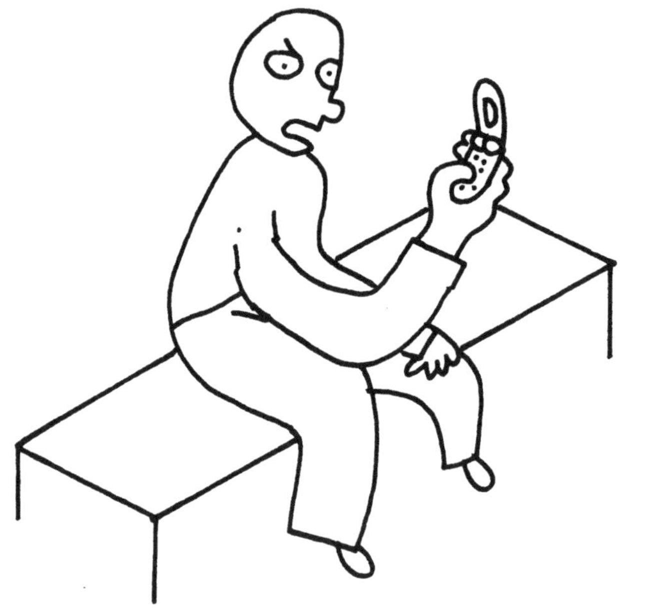

BUT THAT WAS BEFORE I DISCOVERED TEXTING

CRAP TOWNS USA: ALZADA, MT

I was driving through here on a road trip with my uncle and aunt to see the Little Bighorn Battlefield. The town consisted of a gas station, six trailers, some tumbleweeds and the biker bar of all biker bars. The community seemed to be made up entirely of bikers... people who like to feel the wind in their mullets and bugs splatter against their helmetless heads. These people are rebels, people who like to live on the edge, people who like their drinks cheap, their food lousy and their whores a little dirty.

And I present to you a picture of the bar...evidence of why this fair community should receive recognition!

Lindsay O'Brien

I THINK THIS PLACE LOOKS RATHER NICE

THE DEATH OF SPONTANEITY

Crazy Daniel Pemberton has square mates

I have often thought that a good way to judge how in control someone is of their life is their ability to be spontaneous. A truly free person is one with no-one to answer to but themselves. They may have responsibilities, they may have schedules, but these factors do not own them. They do not stick rigidly to a carefully planned rota of life as they are adept at improvising around it. So it has been extremely depressing to discover more and more of my friends and colleagues unable to do anything without a three week warning, preferably backed up with some kind of typed confirmation.

By grudgingly arranging these future rendezvous I am myself stifling my own potential spontaneity. I don't really want to know what I'm doing a month away—in fact I rarely want to know what I'm doing that evening until the time comes. What kind of mood will I be in? What will the weather be like? All these factors play heavily on what would be the most suitable form of entertainment. By creating predefined times and dates for our leisure we are forcing ourselves to act more and more like machines, with allotted times for work and allotted times for play. By pre-arranging dates you raise expectation—every

AARON BURTCH

action has to become a bigger and bigger gesture; if you're planning on cooking a meal you can't just phone someone up and see if they want to help polish off the stuff left lurking in the fridge. You have to prepare a gourmet feast. You can no longer suddenly nip out on a bike ride with someone just because it's a beautiful day—everything has to be organised in advance with appropriate time slots and so on. It drives me round the fucking bend.

Many of the best days or nights I've had have generally been those that were unplanned. The element of surprise is always more enjoyable than that of unfulfilled expectation. With no expectations the only way is up. You realise that you start to gravitate towards like-minded individuals; the continual rebuffing from the diary brigade eventually becomes rather disheartening. People willing to travel on a whim, to alter their daily routine on a phone call, are the ones who excite me most. It's just a shame they seem to be a dying breed.

MANY OF THE BEST DAYS OR NIGHTS I'VE HAD HAVE GENERALLY BEEN THOSE THAT WERE UNPLANNED

THE COCKNEY ALPHABET

by Damien Hirst and Mungo Park

A for 'orses
B for mutton
C for yourself
D for ential
E for she
F for vessant
G for police
H for 'is own
I for Luton
J for oranges
K for the elderly
L for leather
M for sis
N for seema
O for the love of a woman
P for relief
Q for the bus
R for Brick
S for the likes of you
T for dentures
U for mism
V for la france
W for quits
X for liate
Y for mistress
Z for effect

GED WELLS

THE IDLE COOK:

ROADKILL CUISINE

Driving over for dinner

by Rowley Leigh

There are many purported differences between a Frenchman and an Englishman. Take driving. A Frenchman overtakes and then cuts in on his victim with abrupt precision, whilst the Englishman is happy to muddle along in the middle of the road almost interminably. In old age, the process is reversed. Whereas the English geriatric dawdles along in his Austin Metro clinging ferociously to kerb and hedgerow, his French counterpart, dribbling wife by his side, sits proudly on the crown of the road, his *camionette* barring the passage of all behind him. There is one even more crucial distinction between the two nationalities on the road: whereas the Englishman will swerve to avoid hitting wildlife in his path, the Frenchman will swerve to hit it.

MY FRIEND CHRISTIAN SWEARS HE DID NOT SEE THE FIFTY KILO FALLOW THAT HE RAN DOWN IN THE FOREST OF RAMBOUILLET

Of course, there are genuine accidents. My friend Christian swears he did not see the fifty kilo (dressed weight, net of fur and pluck) fallow that he ran down in the forest of Rambouillet one evening. It may have been coincidental that he had some black plastic bin liners in the boot of his beemer—he's quite fussy about his upholstery, is Christian—into which he was able to heave the warm and bleeding carcass. One sure thing is that he had the animal skinned, drawn and hanging in his coldroom before he turned in that night.

To Christian, any other course of action would have been a foolish waste. Jonathan Meades, our leading epicurean, would have agreed with him. For many years, Jonathan's party piece was an extraordinary dish from Elizabeth David called, simply, La Sauce. He cooked this *tour de force* for myself and some colleagues one night. Featuring some shreds of beef, hare, pork, venison and the odd pheasant in an abundance of very rich dark

THE IDLE COOK CONTINUED...

ONE OF MY LESS RESPECTFUL COMPANIONS DUBBED THIS DISH AS "CAR CRASH AND MASH"

sauce and accompanied only by an unctuous potato puree, one of my less respectful companions quickly dubbed this dish as 'car crash and mash', a graphic moniker that did not prevent him from taking three helpings.

Road kill is the new poaching. Apart from a few rogues fishing for wild salmon, no one seriously traps by moonlight these days. The Eddy Grundys of this world collect road kill and the Clarries are still there making rabbit pies and chicken nuggets for the kiddywinks, made with the pheasants that are so plentiful that they cannot be bothered to pluck but are skinned, the breasts removed and the carcass chucked in the bin. Christian would not approve.

CIVET DE GIBIER DES COLLINES RHODANNIENNES

1 hare
1 rabbit
2 pheasant
2 kg shoulder of wild boar
3 onions
3 carrots
6 sticks celery
12 cloves garlic
The peel of an orange
100 peppercorns
4 bay leaves
Several sprigs of thyme
250 ml red wine vinegar
250 ml olive oil
4 bottles Cotes de Rhone villages, Rasteau, Vacqueras, Gigondas or similar
50 grams dried ceps
500 gms unsmoked bacon in a piece
1 kilo pickling onions
250 grams butter

1) Catch the blood and liver from the hare and marinate them in a cup of the vinegar in a small bowl, together with the livers of the rabbit and pheasant. Joint the rabbit, hare and pheasants and place in a large bowl. Cut the boar into large cubes and slice the onions, carrots, celery and garlic and add all to the bowl together with the remaining vinegar, the orange peel, herbs, peppercorns and olive oil. Mix very well before pouring in the wine and marinating in a cold larder for two days.

2) Early on the third day, soak the dried ceps in a cup of cold water. Cut the bacon into lardons, put them in a pan of cold water, bring to the boil and refresh. Soak the pickling onions in a bowl of hot water.

CHLOE KING

Separate the meat, the vegetables and the liquid from the marinade. In a very large copper braising pan, melt a quarter of the butter and brown the drained lardons before adding the vegetables from the marinade. In a separate frying pan, brown the well salted pieces of meat in successive batches of olive oil. Once the vegetables are a golden brown, dust them with a small handful of flour. Once this has been stirred and browned in turn, add all the meat and its juices, the soaked mushrooms and their liquor and the liquid from the marinade. Bring this ensemble gently to the boil and skim off any scum that comes to the surface. Cover the casserole, preferably with a lid sealed with a short crust pastry, and place in a very slow oven for six hours.

3) Peel the pickling onions and brown them very well in butter. Remove the stew from the oven and place it on a gentle heat on top of the stove. The meat should be extremely tender and floating in a dark and unctuous sauce. Add the button onions and let them simmer gently for half an hour. Remove the livers from their vinegar and sear them for fifteen seconds in a very hot frying pan. Pound the livers in a pestle with an equal volume of butter to make a paste and gradually moisten this with the sauce from the casserole. Pour this luxurious *panade* back into the casserole and whisk it to enrich the sauce. Check the seasoning and serve with bread or mashed potatoes.

ENEMY OF IDLENESS:

BILL CULLEN

Shane Hagerty on a dreary Dubliner

Bill Cullen sleeps only five hours a night. He begins each day by staring into the mirror and telling himself twenty times: "I am terrific." Terrifically tired, perhaps.

Bill is an entrepreneur, philanthropist, author and professional Dubliner. But his main mission—which he approaches with evangelical zeal—is to bring this vital message to the world: "Bill Cullen is terrific."

Born in 1942, one of fourteen children, in their one-room dwelling the family had three beds between them. They ate with sharpened spoons, because they couldn't afford knives and forks. They wore potato sacks to keep the rain out and used old newspapers for carpet. As a child, Bill sold fruit with his mammy before becoming a messenger boy in a car dealership at age fourteen. In any article on Bill Cullen, that fact is always followed by this Victor Kiam-esque sentence: "By age twenty-two, he was running the company!"

BILL CULLEN'S NUMBER ONE FAN —BILL CULLEN

He made millions by buying Renault Ireland and today owns a helicopter, flash cars and a mansion. He gives loads to charity and is married to a former model. All of which would be much more admirable if he didn't go on about it so much. His memoir, *It's A Long Way From Penny Apples*, was a nostalgia-sodden account of his rise from terrific street urchin to terrific multi-millionaire. It was his riposte to *Angela's Ashes*: 'I had a miserable Irish childhood too, but I was happy. I pulled myself up by my bootstraps. Even though my family couldn't actually afford bootstraps.'

In a new self-help book, *Golden Apples: Six Simple Steps to Success*, he encourages budding entrepreneurs to be more like him. For instance, by beating the rush hour he gains 7.5 hours a week on the average working man. In his family, no-one was ever allowed a lie-in. "Sleeping is the nearest thing to dying you'll ever do, so don't do too much of it," his granny used to tell him, just before nodding off with exhaustion.

Bill is currently involved in a spat over whether he will become the first Irish astronaut when Virgin Galactic takes off. A counter-claim has come from a chap who made millions from psychic phone lines, so if anyone knows who'll be first you would expect it to be him. But you can see why orbit appeals to Bill. With a new dawn every eight minutes, he'll never be short of the chance to tell himself just how terrific he is.

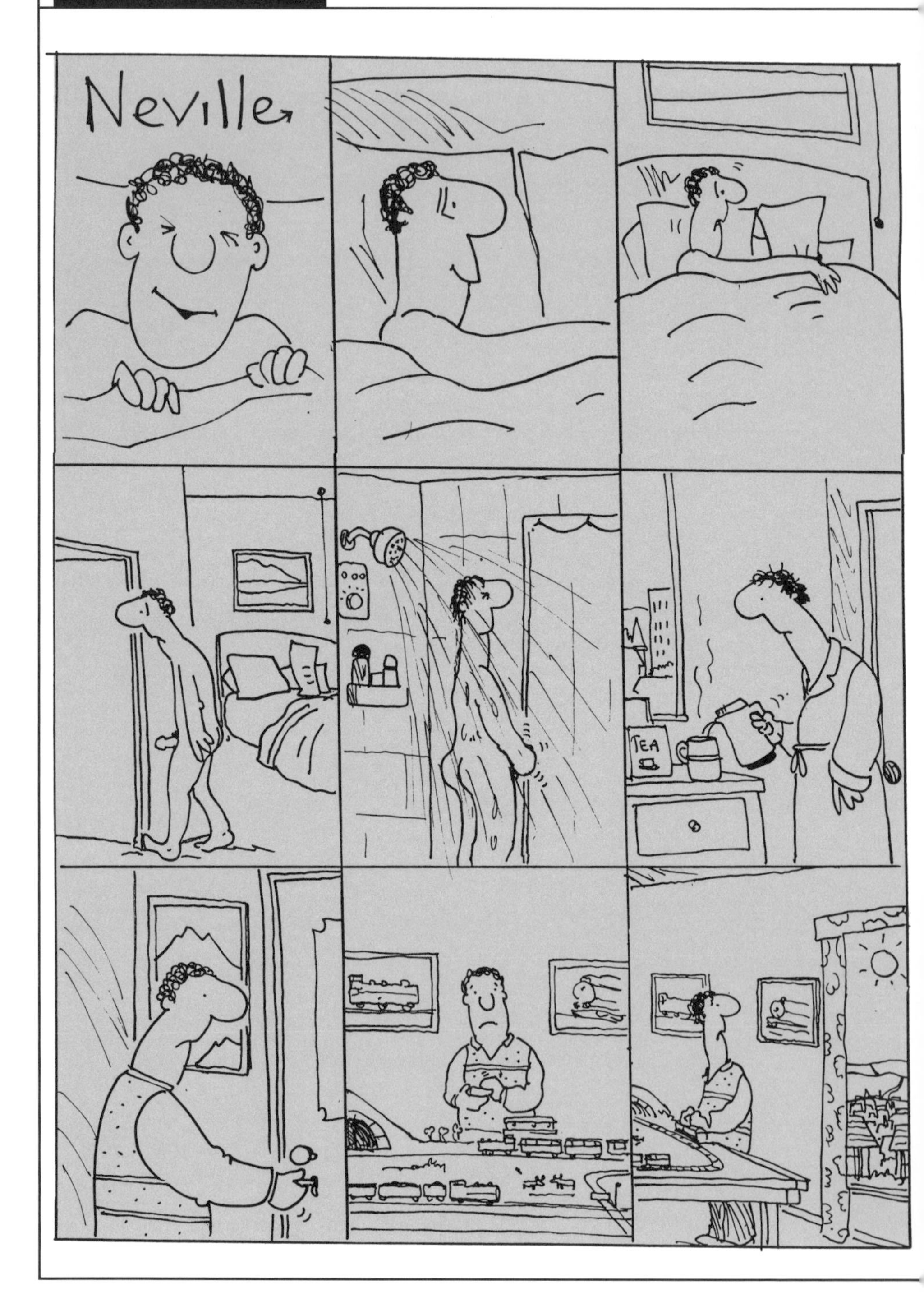
Neville
TEA

THICK BREAD
BUS STOP
BUZZY BUS
for BUZZY BODS
PATH

BUS STOP
TAKE A BUS
KILL
THAT
FUCK OFF

PUB
All bastards are twats
BAR
TAXI
JUST add WATER
COCO
I ♥ NY
Tony Husband
by Tony Husband

BILL AND ZED'S BAD ADVICE

WE'VE FUCKED UP OUR LIVES. NOW IT'S YOUR TURN

DEAR BILL AND ZED,

That capitalist scumbag moneybags Sir Bob Geldof makes me want to puke and I was wondering if you had any Zen wisdom when it comes to things like Live8 and all the rest of that awful tripe?
Grumpy

ZED: Like your dear self, Mr Grumpy, my ire towards this bogus saint, Sir Bob "Gandhi" Geldof, knows no bounds. Suffice herein a few words from a real saint, Matthew to be precise, quoting his boss Sir Jesus no less, on his mount, chapter 6, verses one to four. "Take heed that ye do not your alms before men, to be seen of them. When thou doest thine alms, do not sound a trumpet before thee, as the hypocrites do in the synagogues and the streets, that they may have the glory of men. When thou doest alms, let not thy left hand not know what thy right hand doeth." *Rock on*, The Bible.

BILL: There's much more to be said than what Zed has already said on the subject of Sir Bob but time and space won't allow it here. The Sermon on the Mount covers most of the stuff we should aim to lead our lives by. Geldof sounds like a bit of a yid name, so maybe he's got an excuse 'cos it it wouldn't have been part of his schooling, but his dwarf sidekick Bono has no excuses with all his Bible-bashing. In my eyes, he's a million times worse than Geldof. Someone get me one of those Make Bono History t-shirts. Send it to the Idler, c/o Uncle Bill.

.....

DEAR BILL AND ZED,

I hate sport and therefore I am absolutely aghast at the fact that the great city of hangovers, London, will be hosting the smugfest of the 2012 fascist bodybuilding Olympics. Any advice on what to do with myself when the dark year finally comes?
Dozy

ZED: Bill and I are already planning our own anti-Olympic games with some terrific events. Along with the usual

CHRIS WATSON

Olympian drinking marathons we have devised all manner of other sexy events for the whole family to enjoy. Target shitting, projectile vomiting, speed wanking, a whole rainbow of competitive farting events, volume, tone, follow through; you name it. Do join us, Dozy.
BILL: Yeah, of course we're going to do all that, but the other thing we're planning is a massive bomb at the closing ceremonies. We will be setting up some innocent lads from Leicester to take the fall.

.....

DEAR BILL AND ZED,
Please solve a pub argument. I think roll-ups are best for idlers as they are cheap and fun. But my mate says ready rolled are less grotty and less work as they are ready rolled. What would you two say?
Smokey

ZED: A facetious question, I feel, always deserves a facetious reply. So, you twat, facetiously speaking, I would say that roll-ups always remind me of butch lesbians and malodorous prisons, whilst sleek ready-rolled Dunhills always remind me of Lauren Bacall and Kate Moss. On the other hand, seriously, all fags make me think of smelly, ugly, fast food eating women with revolting teeth and pungent, yeast infections.
BILL: I have never smoked but I do have party trick. My only one. Sadly, it never seems to impress the ladies. It goes like this: I take a lighted cigarette from the mouth of an unsuspecting party guest, I bite off the lighted end and swallow it. I have always found the ready-rolled variety easier on the after-effects. As for lezzas versus Lauren Bacall, give me the lezzas any day, the more clichéd the better. I've always loathed that classic sultry, Hollywood smoking thing.

.....

BILL AND ZED,
Wine or beer?
Boozy

ZED: Boozy, good God, it gets worse. Facetiousness abounds. Well, Mr Boozy, if it's completely wankered that you're aiming for, I would without any hesitation, heartily recommend that you forget alcohol completely and dive into serious solvent abuse. A plastic Tesco's carrier bag, a can of Evo Stik and a secluded spot near a smelly, infested stretch of canal, I find, usually does the trick, you grotty little fucking tramp.
BILL: Wine or beer? Is there no end to the trivial banalities of Idler readers. Even to ask such a question is to insult our wisdom. Is this publication becoming no more than a Parish Pump periodical

BILL AND ZED'S BAD ADVICE CTD...

for those whose hipness has passed its sell-by date but they're still too young for Saga holidays. My advice to you is get a couple of bottles of good claret, a few cans of Stella, pour the lot into a bucket and start drinking.

.....

BILL AND ZED,
I am a writer and would appreciate your advice on whether to use a fountain pen or a biro.
Inky

ZED: Fountain pen absolutely, if your oeuvre is to be displayed for future generations in the autograph section of the British museum. But for you, dear Inky, I suspect that biro would be more than adequate for its lavatory walls.
BILL: A carpenter's pencil does me fine. It appeals to my inner Jesus. Fountain pens just mean you get ink everywhere, and I have always hated those fountain pen ads in the *National Geographic* that attempt to appeal to the worst in male vanity. As fot the British Library, after we have done the Olympics, we're gonna do it, clear the decks of the English literary canon to make way for Zed and myself.

BILL AND ZED,
Coffe or tea?
Sippy

ZED: Bovril, you turd. Fuck, I can't be bollocksed with these arsehole questions anymore. Tea or fucking coffee? What a fucking spaz.
BILL: What has this column come to? We haven't gone through all our years of Zen learning to answer pivling little questions like this. We are the world's premier agony uncles and we expect more. We expect questions of trouble and trauma. We are here to mend broken marriages so that you can go out and break them again. We're here to put the world's rights to wrong. We are here to dance on the graves of the righteous, and help you lose your way.

.....

BILL AND ZED,
What would you do if you had a million pounds?
Penny

ZED: See what I mean? Rip her to shreds Bill.
BILL: I thought long and hard over your question, Penny. The answer I am about to give you is not some ill thought out off-the-cuff-remark. Here goes. If I had one million pounds, I would come round to your house with the lot of fifty quid notes stuffed in a suitcase. I would then sit on your doorstep tearing each and every one in half, shoving the halves with the queen's head on it through your letterbox. I would then take all the other halves and give them to the first bag lady I could find. Both of your lives would be changed. It is for you to work out if the change was for the worse or for the better.

I GOT MY SHIT
TOGETHER!
GWYN
BUT IT WAS
STILL SHIT!

CONVERSATIONS

The End of Work

Anne Celine Jaeger meets Corinne Maier, author of Hello, Laziness and new prophet of Gallic shruggery. Illustrations by Jeff Harrison

Like most people working for a big corporation, Corinne Maier, a 41-year-old economist employed by Electricité de France, was utterly under-whelmed by her job. But unlike the rest of the conformist corporate bods, she actually voiced her frustrations. Not by pulling her line-manager aside during a meeting, or by writing a disenchanted email to the boss. No, Maier went biros 'a-blazing and published a book, which not only ridicules corporate culture but preaches a philosophy of active disengagement as well.

Already a best-seller in France, her 120-page ode to sloth, *Hello Laziness: Why hard work doesn't pay* (*Bonjour Paresse*), is now gaining momentum in the UK. A play on Francoise Sagan's 1950s novel *Bonjour Tristesse, Hello Laziness* is an antidote to the recent assault of career-enhancing self-help books. It's a battle cry for the "neo-slaves" of middle management, which not only outlines why it's in your interest to work as little as possible but also demonstrates how you can corrupt the system from within without appearing to do so.

Unimpressed with the manual, Electricité de France threatened Maier with disciplinary action. The union responded by taking her case to the media on the grounds that the corporation was threatening free speech. The outcome: phenomenal sales, appearances on TV and Maier got to keep her two-day a week job.

Of late, Maier has been sauntering into the EDF offices, knowing full well that she is mocking her employer. Rather than fearing the sack, she is relishing the fact that the tables have turned and that after years of being used by the firm, she can exploit them in return. During her two days in the office, Maier, who is also a trained psychoanalyst, earns enough to live on. She spends the rest of her time dreaming up new book ideas.

IDLER: Was going into conventional business ever a dream of yours?

MAIER: Never. It just sort of happened. I was looking for a job and I found one in a big company and I took it. At first I thought corporations were strange places to be in, and as years passed I realised that working in one was a mistake.

IDLER: When did you first think of subverting the workplace from within?

MAIER: Every day at EDF I saw people who were pretending to work, but who in fact did nothing. There are so many people who do that without even realising they are doing it. They create the impression of being a team-player, they are nice with the managers, they speak the company's jargon etc., but in fact they aren't doing any work. So I thought it would be funny to advise people to pretend to work but to do so consciously.

IDLER: What are your tips for doing this?

MAIER: When they tried to sanction me, my bosses accused me of reading the papers during meetings, but that was wrong. I work part-time, so I don't have to pretend that I'm working as I'm hardly there anyway. I don't pretend. That's one of the reasons they hate me. Nowadays, I do annoy them, but now I don't care what they think because I have enough financial backing thanks to the book. At times, I might have conversations with my colleagues about literature, and they can go on for hours.

IDLER: Why don't you like your job?

MAIER: First of all, I have to go outside. I have to ride my motorbike into the suburbs of Paris and I hate the suburbs. Secondly, I find the building I work in incredibly ugly. It's a depressing place. And thirdly, some of the people I work with are just so uninteresting. Also, I don't get on with my bosses. So I don't like going there. A few years ago, the actual work I did was still interesting because we had to come up with new ways of doing surveys and research. These days, it's all about productivity. We have to do more and more surveys. It's no longer about thinking analytically but about how many surveys you produce–even if these are done badly. It's less intellectually taxing. I have admitted openly in the company for some years now that the only reason I go to work is for the money. But you're not supposed to say that.

IDLER: If you hate it so much, why don't you quit?

MAIER: The fact that I still go there bothers my bosses and I think that's funny. I think that's a good reason to carry on going there. I want to annoy the company that has annoyed me for so long.

IDLER: Don't you think it would be more revolutionary to stop working altogether?

MAIER: I think it's probably more revolutionary to go in and pretend to work. But once I finish my game with EDF I hope I never have to go back to a big company. That's my career plan. At the moment I don't know how that game will end, and when that will be. But I'm curious to find out. I feel like I'm winning by going in. I don't see the point in quitting. It would be more fun to be sacked.

IDLER: What does money mean to you?

MAIER: To me money is important only in the way that it makes you more free in that you're able to say "No" to the things you don't want to do and to people you don't like. I don't care about buying things and showing others that I have money.

IDLER: How do you spend it?

MAIER: At EDF I earn 1500

"I'VE NEVER WANTED TO BE A BOSS. I DON'T LIKE GIVING ORDERS AND TELLING PEOPLE WHAT TO DO"

Euros for 2.5 days a week. That's before tax. I have two kids so of course there are lots of things that need to be paid for. But generally I don't care about consumerist stuff. I have an old motorbike, a 20-year-old car, which doesn't go very fast. Good restaurants are important to me but that's about it.

IDLER: What do you make of the of "working more to spend more" bind?

MAIER: In France we're lucky because we don't even have to think about how we should spend our money. The state helps us spend our money because the taxes are so high. I think it's fine for people to work a lot if they like their job, but if they don't, it's terrible. I just work to eat and to live where I want to live, which is in the 13th arrondissement in Paris, an ordinary neighbourhood.

IDLER: What's the best way you ever spent your money?

MAIER: Paying for my psychoanalyst.

IDLER: How important is status to you?

MAIER: I don't care about status. I've never wanted to be a boss. I don't like giving orders and telling people what to do. I don't care about social status or responsibilities. What I'm interested in is finding new ways of thinking or making things. I don't actually know any people who have a career. They must exist, but I don't know any.

IDLER: To what degree were you inspired by the Situationists and Paul Lafargue?

MAIER: I don't actually like Lafargue's book *The Right to be Lazy*. I think it's written in a really old fashioned style. But I like the idea of defending workers' rights to be lazy. What I like about the Situationists is the way they wrote. Guy Debord had such a beautiful writing style and to me a beautiful style is always revolutionary. They weren't on my mind that much when I wrote *Hello Laziness*, but it's certainly a compliment to be named in the same breath

IDLER: What thinkers inspire you?

MAIER: I like Michel Foucault, particularly his thoughts about power, which he outlines in *Discipline and Punish.* I also like the fact that he was fascinated by the study of marginality. He was interested in crazy people and prisoners. Lacan is another favourite of mine, as is Roland Barthes and Jacques Derrida. I love the French thinkers.

IDLER: How would you describe your philosophy in life?

MAIER: My motto is: "Ne servir à rien, ne servir personne", which translates as "Being useless, slave to no one".

IDLER: But isn't your book useful?

MAIER: Books are not useful. It's important to have books as a collective, but if you think about it, most of them are bad, never read, inaccurate or irrelevant. I would put my book in that category. I'm surprised that people are buying it. I'm disappointed that they are buying this one. I'd much rather they bought my book on Lacan. But I guess the French needed to put a label on something they were suffering from. *Paresse* or laziness is now back in fashion.

IDLER: How has your life changed since the publication of *Hello Laziness*?

MAIER: Ironically, I work much more now than I used to. I do a lot of promotion for the book, so it's good-bye laziness for me. I hope it's temporary. But in some ways I can be more lazy now, as I can say no to things I don't feel like, such as writing books on subjects I don't care about, or making TV programmes with producers I don't like.

IDLER: How has idleness improved your life?

MAIER: I'm only lazy about the things that don't interest me. Laziness is the reverse of desire. When you don't desire something, you don't do it properly and you end up not doing it at all. It's a way of making a distinction between what you want and what you don't want.

IDLER: What do you do in your idle time?

MAIER: To me there is no difference between spare time and real life. So if I have things to do, I do them, and if I don't I think about what I could be writing about. I think the problem for most people is that they don't know what they want. I know that feeling well because I was there myself once. I started seeing a psychoanalyst years ago to deal with that feeling. I was lost. It really helped me find my way. It was a revelation.

IDLER: What's the atmosphere like at the company now?

MAIER: I don't really know. I don't go to meetings any more because I'm not invited. I think my bosses hate me because they think I bite. I'm not kept in the know. And I'm not interested either. If it's changed then it's probably changed for the worse, it might be even more conformist now as they're probably scared to death that another person like me could turn up.

IDLER: How did people at work react to your book?

MAIER: Some people were very nice to me, but the vast majority said nothing at all and some wanted to have me sanctioned.

IDLER: Would you be upset if you got fired in the future?

MAIER: I wouldn't care one bit. Let's see what happens. Something has to happen. I'm waiting for some action. The unions defended me once, but now I think my bosses would be in the right if they sacked me as the situation has changed. Now we don't agree on what I should do. I don't see why I should do something that I'm not interested in and they think that I should obey.

IDLER: How do you deal with status anxiety?

MAIER: I don't suffer from it at all. I see myself as waste, so I really don't care what others think. When you belong to the middle classes, we all live the same way anyway. There's not much to be compared. Psychoanalysis has helped me a lot. When you don't know what you want, you do things and then start thinking it would be important to be richer than the neighbour or have a bigger car etc.

IDLER: Are you any good at doing absolutely nothing?

MAIER: No because I get bored very quickly.

Corinne Maier's Hello Laziness *is published by Orion*

JOE IN HIS YARD AT DEPTFORD

Joe Rush

of the Mutoid Waste Company

Back in 1984 artist and 2000 AD fan Joe Rush and friends had an idea for making sculptures out of old bits of junk. The Mutoid Waste Company was born, and a twenty year adventure involving giant trucks, the collapse of the Berlin Wall, Mig fighters and numerous run-ins with the world's police began. We visited Joe in the yard he now rents in Deptford, to where he'd just returned from a big show at the Glastonbury Festival. We talked about the history of the Mutoids and Joe's creative philosophy.

RACHEL POULTON

IDLER: How did it all start?

RUSH: It started in 1984. I started doing my own work in a little old undertakers' office in a mews in Shepherds Bush. I would spend two weeks on polystyrene carving and working on props, and that paid for me to have my studio.

IDLER: Did you go to art school?

RUSH: No, I learned from my parents who were artists, and from people like Brett Ewins of *2000AD* comic. He started *Deadline*, and was married to my cousin, Victoria. This was when I was 15 or 16. The punk thing had just started and I was well into that... the *2000AD* guys were all ex-skinheads, like Mike Mahone... it was brilliant. When I was 17 I was living with a 28-year-old stripper in Ladbroke Grove, which was quite an education... then we busted up and I didn't know what to do with myself... so I just stuck out my thumb and ended up at the Stonehenge Free Festival. Me and a fella called Willy X were the first two punks to walk on to Stonehenge that year. I spent the summer travelling with the Peace Convoy. Then I came back to

NOTTING HILL CARNIVAL, 2005

NOTTING HILL CARNIVAL

London and was living in a house called Apocalypse Hotel which was in Frestonia in Latimer Road. Then I started putting the Mutoid thing together. I had a nervous breakdown, and quite a lot of things happened. By 1984 I had recovered, and I had discovered that I could make sculpture and I had this style thing going on.

IDLER: How did you come up with the name?

RUSH: I wanted it to be about mutants, people who were suffering from mutation or who were in a state of constant mutation. So "mutoid" came from schizoid or paranoid or mongoloid, and was a description of a person who lives in a state of constant change. In 1985 we built the first truck, in the gardens of this independent state of Frestonia, which was a load of tumbledown houses with the gardens knocked into one. We were the thorn in the side of this hippie utopia with our house. The Clash were photographed outside it; it was quite a wild building. Somebody gave us a burned-out bus, and we turned into it this huge skull with eye sockets that you look through to drive, and with a rib cage done in metal and fibreglass, it was all open air. We were planning to take it to Stonehenge, but while we were building it the Battle of the Beanfield was going on. It became clearer and clearer that we couldn't go there. By the time we crashed out through the fence on this totally wild bit of illegal machinery, we'd decided to go straight to Glastonbury. I think the police thought it was their conscience coming down the road. They just couldn't deal with it, it was so over-the-top and such a heavy image. They just turned their backs. They knew they'd done a wrong thing at Stonehenge.

We got to Glastonbury and I had a massive argument with Michael Eavis. We pulled on with the skull bus towing a big horsebox, with the Ride of the Valkyries playing out of it. We had a totally arsey attitude. We were trying to park up by the main stage. He came over with his radio and I laid into him, he brought over his Hell's Angels security to lean on me, and while they were leaning on me, they saw this centaur coming out of a motorbike, the first Mutoid sculpture I'd ever made, a character built of pistons and levers and engine parts. They were intrigued by it, and said, "what's that on the front of the truck?" And I said, "go and have a look." Suddenly it was just me and Michael Eavis stood on our own again. He found me a space and we did our first shows there.

Then we came back to London and started doing the warehouse parties. We squatted the old Caledonian Road coach station. We had a piece of land in Latimer Road, a bit of nowhere land. Well, we thought it was nowhere land but in fact it was the focus for a lot of business. We ended up getting fire-bombed and I had my skull fractured, and my lung punctured and set on fire and all sorts of shit.

IDLER: Who did it?

RUSH: Well, somebody had a vested interest in getting us off there but as to who, it's not really worth speculating. They didn't actually get us off; what did get us off was the fact that it was fucking wet and rainy and we had no power. We were all sitting there wondering what to do. A lot more had joined because we were under attack. While I'd been in hospital and it was obvious we were going to get hit again, my mate Robin, who was a co-founder of the Mutoids, brilliant man, went out into the street and grabbed everybody who needed a place

"IT WAS TOTAL CHAOS AND THAT WAS THE MAGIC OF IT"

to park up... and that became the Mutoid Waste Company. It was so chaotic... it wasn't people I would have chosen but in actual fact that's what gave the Mutoid thing its flavour. It wasn't really up to anyone to say, "this is my creation". It was total chaos. That was the magic of it; it was creative chaos.

IDLER: How did you fund yourselves?

RUSH: We lived together. We'd give tours. In our Caledonian Road warehouse, we had a river running though the middle. It was actually a flooded drain. We'd built ornamental bridges over it, a forest on one side built out of car exhaust pipes, and gravestones made out of spanners. It was a weird inside-out world. People used to come in and we'd give them the Graveyard Shift, which was a little tour, and then we'd hit them for some money and then we'd got enough money we'd go out and get a bottle of rum or something and all cane that. We lived on scrap metal, we did videos for people. We built stuff for a Frankie Goes To Hollywood video... film companies would do shoots on the sites we were on... we built props for people... and we didn't need much... we were always surrounded by beautiful girls, we always had enough drink and drugs to keep us happy. We managed to eat. We were probably hungry most of the time, but we got on fine.

IDLER: There was never a question of anyone going out to get a job...

RUSH: No, it was full time work, to keep that thing on the road. People did come to help us, but the real hardcore crew had to work very hard. We were getting evicted every three months, which meant we'd have to break everything down, then we'd weigh a lot of it in for the metal.

IDLER: How did you find the places to squat?

RUSH: You'd check places out, get the trucks ready and then a few of you would go on a mission to crack it. To get the locks off, that was the hairy bit. Then suddenly, voom voom voom, all the trucks were in and you'd sit there waiting to see what happened.

IDLER: Were you quite practical anyway, or did you learn by doing it?

RUSH: The original Mutoid thing was probably about four different characters. There was Robin who was a mechanic and an engineer, and myself who was an artist. He had artistic leanings and I had mechanical leanings. So we crossed over. There was another man called Ricky Lee, who was a gypsy who used to run a scrap truck. He taught us about scrap metal.

IDLER: Was the idea of using waste a deliberate philosophical thing or did it just happen?

RUSH: No, it was more to do with the randomness of the objects. With waste, you can get something that's been beautifully manufactured, but which has no further use and which can be a lovely object. A spring or a bit of chain is actually a really lovely thing, and done right, it can look like the most beautiful piece of jewellery. People said we were talking about environmental issues, but in truth, we weren't. That wasn't our message. Our

ANDRZEJ LIGUZ / MOREIMAGES.NET

EXHAUST PIPE CHANDELIER, GLASTONBURY

INSECT

DINOSAUR

message was: be creative. And create just for the fun of creating, for its own sake, don't get hung up on whether you are an artist or not.

IDLER: The objection I get when I raise these issues is: it's all right for you creative people. What about the people who aren't creative? What will they do in your idlers' world? Well, surely everyone is creative.

RUSH: Yes, but the team I've got here... Terry there has a brilliant eye for scrap, Tony there is a brilliant engineer and welder. It would be no good if we were all three artists... on the scale we're working at, we need these different talents. We're all quite happy with our talents. What it is, you're gifted; these things are your gifts. It is a gift to you, to be creative or to be able to hear music in your head and interpret it or to take a photograph. Whether you choose to sell your gifts or work out what value they've got on the market is neither here nor there. You run the risk of jeopardizing your gift by prostituting it. It is your gift; it's given to you as a present. I think people get confused by that one. If there's anyone sitting there getting jealous about it, it means they're not really gone out and looked for what their gift is...

IDLER: But the current set-up, the job system and industrial system, doesn't offer people the chance to find their gift.

RUSH: No, it doesn't. In fact, it actively discourages it. But people bind to that because they want the easy life. Right now, what we're doing really works. But there have been long periods of hungry, fucked up, argumentative times and I've wondered why we've kept on doing it. It's much easier to let somebody else do the thinking, take home your regular wage and sell your life off piecemeal. Everybody, I think, gets the sense that there's another world out there, but when you start to get into that world, it raises a lot of questions about what you've been told. You can start to get vertigo, you suddenly realise, you have to rethink everything. Most people scuttle straight back and never poke their head above the wall again.

IDLER: I have found that, once you start questioning the world of jobs, then all the other structures seem to be similarly unhelpful to living.

RUSH: I think the saddest thing is when people work all their life, sorting away their bit of pension, just to find that somebody's run wild with it and lost it all. To feel that you've been ripped off in that way at that stage of your life is a terrible thing to take to your grave, I think. But you can see that clearly in Wall Street: when Wall Street crashed, all these people came to the banks to cash in their life savings, and the money wasn't there, the bank was shut.

IDLER: Money is just a balancing act.

RUSH: Money is just a creative idea, like anything else. People with a lot of money understand that.

IDLER: So... you were real pioneers of the warehouse party scene.

RUSH: Yeah, we were right early with that. By accident. We squatted the Kings Cross Coach Station, and these boys came in, and said, "oh, we were going to do a party here." And we went, "oh, we'll do a party with you." They provided the sound system and the music and did the advertising, they were called C3P. And we decorated the place up... we cut the tops of cars and put them in the drain to make it look really deep and somebody got a motorboat and

VOLKSWAGEN DINOSAUR

FLOATING BOAT AT GLASTONBURY, 2005

put that in there and someone else made a water-skier on ironing boards... we had this giant frogspawn from a film set and it got wilder and wilder and madder and madder... the first party we did we had around four or five hundred people... the week after about nine hundred and the week after that we had to throw the doors open because people were being crushed.

IDLER: And all these things were completely illegal?

RUSH: Totally.

IDLER: So you needed a lot of courage...

RUSH: When we were building our skull bus, people said to us, "you'll never get this anywhere... as soon as you take it on the road, you'll get nicked. It's got no windows, the steering wheel is just a bit of wire, it's got no tax, no insurance..." But we carried on doing it in the face of all of this. Every time it got impounded, we got it back. We parked outside Buckingham Palace, we drove to Scotland and back. Our attitude to it was, the thing is so obviously illegal, that people will think it must be legal. We had a technique that the gypsies taught us, The Mumble, is always having a explanation as to why you're in this vehicle.

IDLER: What's an example of it?

RUSH: Well, when Frank was on his way back from Glastonbury, the police stopped him and said, "Is this your vehicle?" And he said, "Don't talk to me about this vehicle, I've had it up to here with this thing! They sent me to Glastonbury to pick up the stage... and look at it... it's got no fucking windows, it's got no roof! I'm going to get it back to the depot and I never want to see the cunting thing again." And the copper goes, "Good luck, you'd better get on your way." And that's The Mumble. You're always on your way to somewhere just out of their area, you're doing a kids' show, or it's on the way to the scrapyard. It's the nature of a policeman's mind that he works within a certain framework of rules. The other thing is that we really weren't a threat to anyone. And the police were quite impressed. Other people running warehouse parties would bar their doors to the police. But we would bring them in and show them around, just as though they were normal people. By the time they were half way round, they were talking about stuff in the same way any other punter would... we treated them as individuals.

IDLER: So you don't have an aggressive "them and us" attitude towards police?

RUSH: No, not at all. Because I don't think it is "them and us", I think it's just us. And the further I've gone on in life, the more I've realised that's true. At that time we believed we were an alternative society. But now I think that actually we're just a part of society and people like us have always existed. For us to go around saying we are an alternative society is a cop-out.

IDLER: You're the crazy guys coming into town, the troubadors.

RUSH: Yes, that's who we are. When we got to Europe, we didn't have the legacy of the Peace Convoy or the warehouse parties or the punk anarchy thing. They saw us for what we are, which is artists and showmen.

IDLER: And when was that?

RUSH: When ecstasy came in, our thing was a bit superfluous. People didn't need the big sculptural stuff to trip them out... just a strobe light and a beat... Also, we had always wanted to go abroad... so we got in the trucks and moved to

Amsterdam, to a giant squatted island. Some English types had built a bar out of two buses... they did a festival and invited us out there. We built Stonehenge out of cars... that was our introduction to Europe. In England, we'd been getting so closed down, the police were pursuing us across counties... helicopters...

IDLER: That was Major's government, wasn't it?

RUSH: Yeah, one of the fuckers.

IDLER: But soon after that he started taking credit for the new creativity and "Cool Britannia".

RUSH: I hate the lot of them. I hate politicians. There is something suspect about someone who wants to be in a position to tell other people what to do... so from Amsterdam we went down into West Berlin when it was a walled city. We drove 200 miles through the Eastern Bloc, a huge convoy of bizarre vehicles, mutated trucks and vans, workshops.

IDLER: Was Ken Kesey an influence?

RUSH: Funnily enough I never read that until much later on, but when I read it I realised that we were a continuation of that. West Berlin was incredible. We built this giant man leaning over the Berlin Wall: his chest was a Volkswagen Beetle and his feet were bathtubs, and he was on railway tracks, leaning out of the station which had been bombed in the Kreuzberg, a really radical area. They thought we were building a rocket launcher to go through the wall. The Mayor of West Berlin, the Major of East Berlin, the American forces' representative in West Berlin, the Russian military representative in East Berlin, all of them came to Robin and told him that they didn't want this gift. He is so pig-headed, that he did it anyway. And three months later, the wall was down... I ain't saying we brought the wall down, but we sensed that chaotic edge... our man was a great smiley geezer, and in his hands was a giant chrome bird made of exhaust pipes called the Silver Bird of Peace. Finally we went to Italy for a theatre festival in a village called Santarchangelo. They liked what we were doing because they're really into their machines... they loved the supercharged tractors with rhinoceros heads on them and motorbikes with tractor wheels on them. We had to do parades in the town, so we all drove in with wellington boots on our heads, riding motorbikes with caterpillars on them, three-wheelers with aircraft wings on them... they just loved it. At the end we said, "do you mind if we stay on for a few weeks?" They said, "if you ask us, we'll have to say no, so don't ask us." Ten years later, the site's still there.

I eventually went back to Berlin, when the wall came down. I thought, "I've got to get some of this." It was the fucking biggest scrap pile on the planet. By the end we had two Mig 21 fighter planes, which we'd robbed off the airports. We built Stonehenge out of Russian armoured personel carriers and tanks. The Russians were trying to get rid of this stuff and we were having the time of our lives, finding big eight wheel drive all terrain vehicles, in an old orchard, whacking batteries on them, writing our own number plates and just driving them straight into the middle of Berlin. Everything in East Germany was state-owned. When it collapsed, they just got out of their combine harvester in the field and walked away from it. They left all their tools on the factory bench and walked away. There were Trabants everywhere, full size road diggers–we

ANDRZEJ LIGUZ / MOREIMAGES.NET

ANDRZEJ LIGUZ / MOREIMAGES.NET
RACHEL POULTON

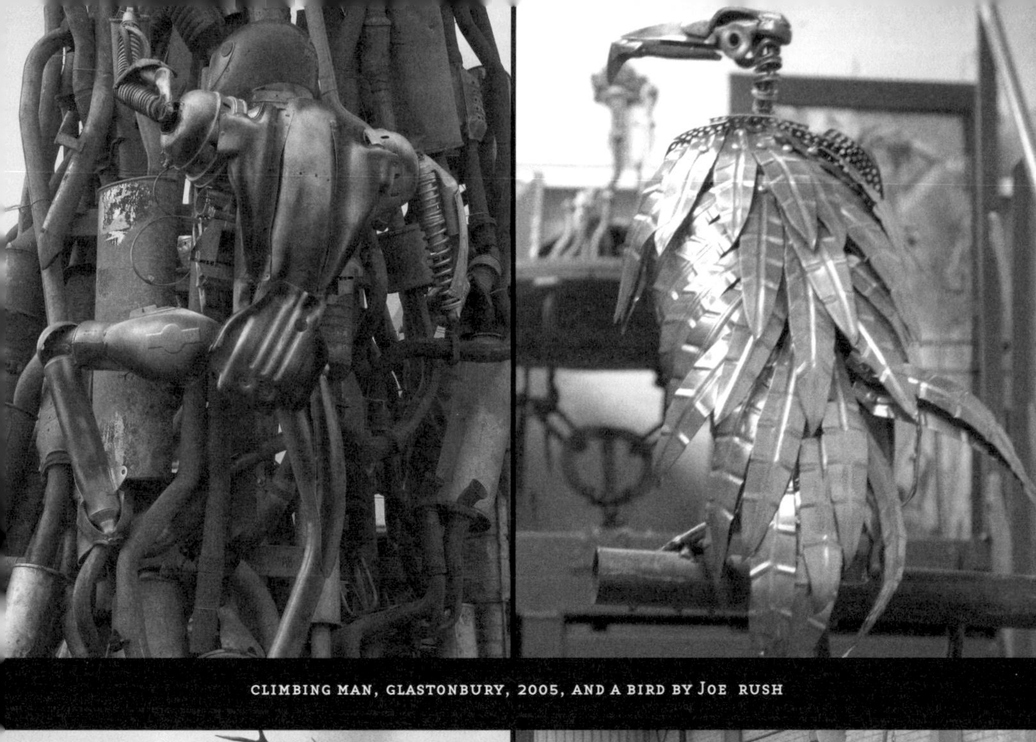

CLIMBING MAN, GLASTONBURY, 2005, AND A BIRD BY JOE RUSH

just brought it all in.

IDLER: And how were you funding yourselves?

RUSH: Well, we ran a bar in Berlin called House of Fear. We did it up with iconic Russian paintings, soldiers with missiles and sunplashes. The tables were made out of bombs, the bar was the front of a Russian truck, we put netting around it. After that I took the Mig fighters up to Potsdammerplatz and we started a big sculpture garden there. Eventually Spiral Tribe came to Berlin. We got on very well. We took the Migs to the Czech republic.

IDLER: How do you transport a Mig fighter?

RUSH: There's a whole book there! We had a huge transporter trailer that steered front and back, it had sixteen wheels, and we had a massive Russian truck. The police roadblocked us as soon as we got out of Berlin but after a bit they just couldn't deal with it and they had to let us go. But it was the onset of winter, my girlfriend was pregnant, so I cut loose, jumped in a little truck and went down to Italy and the first child was born down there. He was born with a heart defect which meant that we had to stay close to a hospital. I started a thing called Mutech, a mixture between the Spirals and the Mutoids. It was a whole stage show with acrobats, dancers, drummers, video, sculptures, the lot, which was something I'd always wanted to do. We'd always had the feeling that we could transpose this chaotic thing into a tangible show that would say something very clear, and we did actually achieve that. Once I'd done it, though, it was pretty impractical to keep doing all that, on no budget, while trying to bring up two kids. I sold all the trucks and trailers, and moved back to England to be nearer a hospital. Now I've slowly started again. But instead of doing the huge great travelling thing, I work more on fine sculpture, and do big events like Glastonbury or Notting Hill Carnival.

FEATURES

Sir John Bond
Group Chairman, HSBC

The Culture of Credit

EDWARD CHANCELLOR ON HOW NEVER-NEVER MONEY FUELS THE FANTASY ECONOMY. ILLUSTRATIONS BY JOE HARRISON

Only official publications of international organizations, such as the World Bank or the IMF, continue to refer to the world's richest countries as the "industrial economies". Nowadays, the West, or more precisely the Anglo-Saxon economies of Britain and the United States, make hardly anything that you can touch or feel. Occasionally, you might pick up a match-box and read with surprise, the once familiar legend, "Made in England". But this is probably just a marketing trick. The same is true of the United States, where flashy cars today are simply referred to as "imports."

How should one characterize the economy in our post-industrial age? Look-ahead types will say we belong to a "service economy" comprised of "knowledge workers". But this is an even greater lie. If you don't believe this, then pick up the telephone and try and call any business you care–your insurance or telephone company, say–and see if you can get anything resembling service. If you're lucky you will wait half an hour before a well-meaning but uncomprehending Indian, sitting in an air-conditioned office in Bangalore, picks up the phone. The trains don't run on time. The Royal Mail mislays your post. Plumbers are famously difficult to track down and, when found, expensive, incompetent and dishonest. Welcome to the modern service economy.

Marxists would say we say the distinction between the industrial and the service economy is artificial: we live in a capitalist economy. Yet this proposition is even more quaint. Capital, as Marx and Engels, knew it was derived from savings and used to build satanic mills where the proletariat could be exploited. But we no longer build factories and have recently given up saving. A silent revolution has taken place: Capitalism is

Maarten Van Den Bergh
Chairman, Lloyds TSB Group plc

dead. So how can it be that if we no longer earn our keep by making things that other people want, that we live better than ever?

Think for a minute. You live in a house, but you didn't pay for it. And you probably didn't pay for your car, TV, washing-machine, or even your most recent holiday. You may even be quite rich, but you never put a penny away. How did you achieve this miraculous feat? You have lived on credit. Easy money has fueled a housing boom, turning homes into pension funds and current accounts; enabling people to cash in their home equity and spend beyond their means. You live in your house, you live off your house. Household borrowing has grown three times faster than income in recent years. What this means is that for every £4 of fresh expenditure, three of them have been borrowed. England is a nation of Micawbers: our expenditure exceeds our means. But whereas Dickens" amiable spendthrift found this to be a miserable condition, we are outwardly contented and will remain that way as long as the credit spigot is turned on.

In theory, the financial system exists to shuffle savings to those parts of the economy where they can best be used. The reality of our modern economy is that finance exists as an end in itself. Last year, American financial institutions earned nearly half of all the profits generated by the private sector. The most profitable companies today are banks. They account for roughly a quarter of the value of the stock market in both London and New York. Employment in the financial sector provides work for ever larger number of people. The bloated bonuses of investment bankers and hedge fund managers trickle down through the economy to sustain restaurateurs, car salesmen, art dealers, swimming-pool builders, nannies and, one way or another, the rest of us. Mortgage loans provide for builders, DIY merchants, electricians, furniture retailers and infamous plumbers. America may recently have lost millions of manufacturing jobs but now finds work for more than a million estate agents or realtors. Hundreds of millions of credit card solicitations are sent out each year, offering hundreds of billions of pre-approved loans. The advertising slogans of the card issuers are the commandments of our age: "Don't put it off, put it on," "Live Richly', "Long Live Dreams," "Live in the Moment," "It's everywhere you want to be'…

The world's sole superpower is also the world's largest debtor-nation. The United States owes tens of trillions of dollars to foreign creditors. Each year, thanks to its ever increasing trade deficit, the US becomes more in hock to the rest of the world. Today, foreigners own more than half of the outstanding US national debt. They supply the means for Americans and British to live beyond their means. Goods are made in China and bought on credit supplied by China. A post-modern economic irony: prosperity in the nominally capitalist United States of America is underwritten by loans from the nominally communist People's Republic. The much-trumpeted success of the US and UK economies has little to do with liberalization, free markets and the supposed flexibility of the work-force: the Anglo-Saxon economic model is just a well-oiled credit machine.

Although credit dominates our lives few people appear to understand it. Economists are little help in this matter. They have reduced credit to what they call risk. This risk has been quantified, measured, correlated, sliced and diced, distributed, hedged, guaranteed, insured, and generally played around with until it eventually turns into something like a certainty. Somewhere in the process, credit appears to have been forgotten about. This is not surprising, since current economic orthodoxy follows the teaching of monetarists, such as Milton Friedman, Mrs. Thatcher's spry guru. The monetarists, as their name suggests, believe money to be all important.

They are mistaken: money doesn't exist any longer. It is just another form of credit. In the days when gold was money, bank-notes were referred to as "paper credit". Bank-notes today count as money but are they any less credit? Today's money is an entry in an electronic ledger. Your money is the bank's liability, matched by an asset, in the form of a loan to somebody else. When you spend money, the credit shuffles round the system. Here is not the place for an economic disquisition. I merely want to show that credit is largely ignored and misunderstood by modern economists.

If we want to discover genuine insights into the nature of credit, the best place to start, in my view, is with the works of those early eighteenth century writers who chronicled the birth of a commercial society in Britain. When William of Orange usurped his father-in-law's throne a little over three centuries ago, he brought with him the practitioners of "Dutch finance': stockbrokers and bankers, projectors of joint-stock companies and insurers, double-entry bookkeepers, innovative issuers of bills and bonds, of annuities and lotteries. In a world where money was always in short supply, credit pervaded all transactions. Contemporaries observed the evolution of an economy which was no longer agricultural but was not yet industrial. In other words, they saw an economy which had much in common with our own.

No one tried harder to capture the essence of this new economy, than Daniel Defoe. Defoe saw credit performing the role that Adam Smith would later ascribe to self interest. Credit was difficult to perceive or even describe: "By this Invisible, Je ne scay Quoi, this Non-natural, this Emblem of a something, tho" in it self nothing, all our War and all our Trade is supported," wrote Defoe. Time again, this most commercially aware of English novelists wrestled with the mysteries and paradoxes of credit. He prefaced his Essay Upon the Loans (1710) with the following words:

I am to speak of what all People are busie about, but not one in Forty understands... If a Man goes about to explain it by Words, he rather struggles to lose himself in the Wood, than bring others out of it. It is best describ'd by it self; "tis like the Wind that blows where it lists, we here the sound thereof, but hardly know whence it comes, or whither it goes.

Like the Soul in the Body, it acts all Substance, yet is it self Immaterial; it gives Motion, yet it self cannot be said to Exist, it creates Forms, yet has itself no Form, it is neither Quantity or Quality; it has no Whereness, or Whenness, Scite, or Habit. If I should say it is the essential Shadow of something that is Not; should I not Puzzle the thing rather than Explain it, and leave you and my self more in the Dark than we were before.

Understood or not, Defoe recognized that it was credit which "gives Life to Trade, gives Being to the Branches, and Moisture to the Root; "tis the Oil of the Wheel, the Marrow in the Bones, the Blood in the Veins, and the Spirits in the Heart of all Negoce, Trade, Cash and Commerce in the World."

Some of Defoe's contemporaries also understood credit to be mainspring of prosperity. Sir Richard Steele, for instance, produced an economic allegory for the readers of the *Spectator*. Steele described entering a Palace of Vanity, whose dome "bore so far the resemblance of a Bubble', where enthroned Vanity was attended by Ostentation, Self-Conceit, Flattery, Affectation, and Fashion. When Broken Credit appears alongside Folly, there is consternation, and the visitor, "plainly discern'd the Building to hang a little in the Air without any real Foundation… But as they begun to sink lower in their own Minds, methought the Palace sunk along with us, till they arrived at the due point of esteem which they ought to have of themselves; then part of the building in which they stood touched the earth."

Steele has observed something very important: credit provides the bootstraps by which the economy holds itself up. When those bootstraps break, the economy comes crashing to the ground.

Where did Credit spring from? Defoe answered that it came from the "Conduct and Just Behaviour" of men. It was founded upon mutual confidence, trust, honesty, just and honourable dealing, punctuality and general probity. Credit belonged to the world of the merchant not the aristocrat. It "never was chain'd to Mens Names," wrote Defoe, "but to their Actions; not to Families, Clans, or Collections of Men; no, not to Nations; "Tis the Honour, the Justice, the Fair-Dealing and the equal Conduct of Men… that raise the thing call'ed Credit among them; wheresoever this is found, CREDIT will live and thrive, grow and encrease."

This was only a half truth. In his novels Defoe revealed a more complicated world. Credit was founded upon character. However, a person's true character is not always easy to discern. In an urban world, many people are unknown. In such

MONEY DOESN'T EXIST ANY LONGER — IT IS JUST ANOTHER FORM OF CREDIT

a society, false identities can be adopted and used to gain access to credit. Defoe's Moll Flanders, for instance, is constantly assuming new identities and hiding her true character and history as a whore, bigamist and thief. In Defoe's works, any villain might procure credit under false pretences by adopting a gentlemanly air and a fine frock coat.

In the beginning, credit was more easily acquired by persons of rank, who inherited the credit of their forefathers. Georg Simmel in *The Philosophy of Money* (1907) cited an English businessman's remark that "the common man is one who buys goods on cash payment; a gentleman is one to whom I give credit and who pays me every six months with a cheque." The snobbery of credit endured a very long time. Many merchant banks lost money in 1974 as a result of the crisis triggered by the collapse of the *arriviste* finance house, Slater Walker. The head of Lazard Brothers, Lord Poole, asked how his firm had avoided being damaged by the fall of the new financiers. "Quite simple," Poole replied, "I

Sir George Mathewson
Chairman, The Royal Bank of Scotland Group

only lent money to people who had been at Eton."

Marx described the capitalist economy as revolving around a cash nexus, a faceless system of exchange. This is a double fiction. First, as Defoe and many others recognized, credit, not cash, characterized the post-feudal economy. Secondly, the credit economy abhors anonymity. It can only grow by gathering, and assessing, more and more personal information about character and identity. Not everyone could afford to be as exclusive to Lord Poole. There were insufficient Old Etonians to go round. Besides, some of them might be rogues and others imposters.

Initially, a rather crude solution was found to the problem of mistaking character. Creditors were empowered to imprison delinquent debtors. By the early nineteenth century, there were more debtors than felons in British gaols (a fact explained partly by the preference of the criminal justice system for deportation and capital punishment rather than imprisonment). It was widely believed that but for the sanction of prison, the system of credit would break down, since debtors–Etonians possibly excepted–might be expected to walk away from their dues. However, jailing debtors was an expensive and inefficient way of maintaining the credit system. Besides, the squalid condition of many debtors' jails provoked a public uproar. Palgrave's Dictionary (1891) suggested that the threat of jail encouraged tradesmen to provide credit without heed, or false credit, as it was known: "If a man has neither property nor character," opined Palgrave, "it is better that he should not be able to obtain credit by what is practically a mortgage on his body."

Character could not infallibly be judged by dress or bearing. In order to flourish, the credit economy required institutions for the surveillance of character. These were provided initially by the tradesmen's associations. In 1776, there was founded in London a body which called itself "The Guardians, or The Society for the Protection of Trade against Swindlers and Sharpers." Its members paid a guinea a year for access to the records of fraudulent customers and assistance in pursuing them. Trade protection societies proliferated in the following century, their newsletters providing descriptions of swindlers who assumed genteel appearance and fake connections in order to acquire credit. Tradesmen testifying before a select committee in 1823 warned of identity theft. False credit was being obtained by "people that pass for gentlemen at different places... and make use of gentlemen's names behind their backs." By the late nineteenth century the National Association of Trade Protection Societies had developed a "telegraphic code" to disseminate information on credit risk: its members were informed whether prospective customers were "safe', "good', to be handled "with care" or merely "moderate".

The estimation of character in the United States, a nation of immigrants spreading out across a continent, was an even more challenging task. Yet from the moment the pilgrim fathers landed on Plymouth Rock, bearing a "heavy burthens" of debt, which they arranged to pay off in annual "estallments', the American experiment has always remained a speculation financed with credit.

The immigrant dwellers of New York's Hell's Kitchen, living off the retail credit of the

"Borax" stores (Borax is a native salt of boron, used widely as a detergent. Borax here is a corruption of borgs, the Yiddish for credit. Shopping at a Borax store was said to "clean a person out."). The prospectors of the Yukon had their purchases entered into the credit ledger of the local dry goods store, to be redeemed when gold was struck. The Boston bourgeoisie "got trusted" and had their pianos and much else on account. The plungers on the stock market gamed with margin loans from their brokers.

"Beautiful credit! The foundation of modern society," wrote Mark Twain in *The Gilded Age* (1870), "Who shall say that this is not the golden age of mutual trust, of unlimited reliance upon human promises? That is a peculiar condition of society which enables a whole nation to instantly recognize point and meaning in the familiar newspaper anecdote, which puts into the mouth of a distinguished speculator in lands and mines this remark: "I wasn't worth a cent two years ago, and now I owe two millions of dollars."

At times the young American states, like some emerging market economies today, endangered their credit by repudiating their debts. In the early 1840s, some nine states stopped payment of interest on their bonds; prompting the Rev. Sydney Smith, a suffering investor, to pen his "Humble Petition to the House of Congress at Washington" in which he warned that "a great nation...[had become] unstable in the very foundations of social life, deficient in the elements of good faith." Credit faltered more frequently in the private sphere. In Walden, Henry Thoreau famously observed that among all merchants "a very large majority, even ninety-seven in a hundred are sure to fail." Leaving behind, no doubt, a pile of unpaid debts.

In his original and engaging *Born Losers: A History of Failure in America* (recently published by the Harvard University Press), Scott Sandage takes up Max Weber's idea that capitalism is a system which forces the individual "insofar as he is involved in the system of market relationships, to conform to the capitalistic rules of practice." No rules of practice are more demanding than those of credit, for they don't demand merely demand conformity from the individual, they seek to govern his soul. In the United States character became shaped by the demands of the creditor.

The creditor has always taken a prying interest in the lives of his debtors. In his *Advice to a Young Tradesman* (1748), Benjamin Franklin averred that: "The most trifling Actions that affect a Man's Credit, are to be regarded. The Sound of your Hammer at Five in the Morning or Nine at Night, heard by a Creditor, makes him easy Six Months longer. But if he sees you at a Billiard Table, or hears your Voice in a Tavern, when you should be at Work, he sends for his Money the next Day. Finer Cloaths than he or his Wife wears, or greater Expence in any particular than he affords himself, shocks his Pride, and he duns you to humble you. Creditors are a kind of People, that have the sharpest Eyes and Ears, as well as the best Memories of any in the World."

In the following century, it became the profitable task of credit agencies to serve as the eyes and ears of creditors across the nation. The first credit bureau, the Mercantile Agency, was established in the mid-nineteenth century by Lewis Tappan, a temperance advocate and evangelical anti-slaver. His agency promised to sell "information with the regard to the credit and affairs of every man in business." Two decades later, the Mercantile was gathering some seventy thousand reports a year, detailing the public and private lives of the country's small traders.

Businessmen were "watched" by the firm's scattered agents, who gathered together what could be gathered of their history, current position and future prospects. If a person was found wanting in the three Cs–capital, character and capacity, credit would be withdrawn. According to Sandage, the agency rated men as commodities: ranging from "as good as gold" to "bad eggs," who were "good for nothing." In time, this gave way to quantification of men's character: good credits were classed as "A1" where the letter stood for capital and the number for ability.

Tappan's purpose in founding the business was not purely commercial, he had a mission: the systematic verification of credit, he believed, would revitalize moral responsibility in commerce rewarding men of integrity and punishing the lazy, the rash, and the dishonest. He boasted that his firm "checks knavery, and purifies the business air." The reports approved of certain character traits: it was good to be disciplined, industrious, "careful', "prompt," and "pushing." Bad credit might result from being "over-pushing" or over-trusting in your business life or be given to "fast-living', gaming, women-chasing, or otherwise dissolute behavior in your private life. One report commented, "if it be true that he drinks he will fail.") The barrier between private and public became blurred by the credit agency's relentless pursuit of character.

According to Sandage, credit agents were disciplinarians: "the system institutionalized moral judgment–making such judgment a vital business tool and recruiting agents to supply it." Both success and failure were deemed to reflect man's moral character rather than the unpredictable vicissitudes of the market. The credit agency, in Sandage's words, became a "panopticon without walls', "an organized system of espionage', according to a contemporary, where moral judgment and commercial reason coalesced. By his lonely pond, near Concord, Massachusetts, Thoreau despaired of this cold-blooded rating of men's souls: "We falsely attribute to men a determined character–a putting together of all their yesterdays–and averaging them–we presume to know them."

THE CREDITOR HAS ALWAYS TAKEN A PRYING INTEREST IN THE AFFAIRS OF HIS DEBTORS

The credit agency in the nineteenth century, as Sandage points out, was an "information system". It sought to apprise those details of character and identity in a rapidly expanding nation which might have been readily available in a more parochial world, a vanished place where the creditor knew you, "by the sound of your hammer." Today, our world is even more fragmented, evolving and complex. If you live in a large city, it is likely you don't know anything about your neighbour, except perhaps his face; and even that may change every year or so, as people move on, trade up, drop out.

It's hard to believe that credit can continue expanding in a world where nobody knows anyone, yet it does. Measured as a multiple of incomes,

NEW RANGE OF IDLER T-SHIRTS IS AVAILABLE

AT WWW.IDLER.CO.UK

household credit climbs to a new peak, year after year; defying predictions of doom, as it soars to fresh heights. We live in the age of instant credit. No longer must you wait two weeks for the bank manager to approve a car loan, you can have it in minutes, even seconds. It's tempting to consider the deluge of credit card solicitations, with offers of pre-approved credit limits, as insincere, like the marketing bumpf that was mailed by Reader's Digest, instructing you dial some number to collect your £50,000 prize.

Credit card companies, you have never heard of, really want to lend you money. Why? Because they already know you. How do they know you? Because the credit bureaus today, the descendants of Lewis Tappan's Mercantile Agency, are more powerful and more intrusive than ever before. Whereas Tappan sought to survey just the business class and his agents were able to gather together only a limited amount of information, the modern credit bureaus collect information on everyone and have the capacity to collect unlimited data on those they spy upon.

Contemporary credit agencies piece together your credit history from a variety of sources: they know how long you have lived at your current address, whether you have ever been declared bankrupt or if there are any county court judgements against you; they know how many cards and accounts you have, how often you apply for credit, the extent of your credit line; they know whether you pay bills late and if you default on debts.

The data in your credit history are known as "characteristics". These are fed into a computer which searches for correlation with default, coming up with a credit score. The score being an evaluation of character suitable for an information age; an assessment of the mathematical probability of loss. In the interests of speed and breadth of coverage, the commoditization of a borrower's character, begun by the nineteenth century credit ages, has ended in digitalization. Your credibility measured in three figures.

What businesses do with the credit score depends on regulation. In the United States, there are few restrictions on its application. It is used in marketing, in loan approvals and pre-approvals, and in deciding what interest rate to charge customers. It is also used as a proxy for character in areas unrelated to acts of borrowing. Employers and landlords use credit scores for job applicants and tenants. Insurers use them to determine premiums and coverage for auto and home insurance. Utilities use credit scores in deciding whether to provide services. One Texan energy company recently decided to vary its electricity rates in line with customers" credit score.

The rewards are great for those with the best credit scores. In the United States, lenders provide them with larger loans, at lower interest rates, with smaller down-payments. Borrowers with high scores qualify for "no income" and "no document" loans. In other words, they are happy to know nothing about you apart from your score. It used to be that success or failure determined your access to credit. Access to credit in the era of low interest rates and booming house prices now determines success or failure. "Remember," said the wise Franklin, "credit is money."

Back to the Land

Andy Worthington uncovers a tradition of radical land reform movements from the 17th century Diggers to the present day. Illustrations by Bill Sanderson

Dreams of Utopia–and specifically of communal living, self-sufficiency and equality–have arisen throughout British history at times of extraordinary social upheaval, and have always drawn ferocious opposition from the land-owning establishment. The first bold attempt at instigating land reform and redressing the disparity between the rich and the poor was forged in the civil war of the 1640s by a group whose name still resonates over 350 years later: the Diggers, founded by Gerrard Winstanley.

Winstanley was a wool trader whose business was ruined in the early years of the Civil War. After moving to Surrey, he became an agricultural labourer and an avid pamphleteer with a visionary agenda of radical land reform. In "The New Law of Righteousness", published in January 1649, Winstanley identified private property as "the curse and burden the creation groans under", and urged the poor to rise up–with spades rather than weapons–and take back the land that had been violently taken from them by the ruling classes, who had kept it through repressive legislation backed up by the corruption of the church. By May 1649, when the execution of Charles I seemed only to have replaced one tyrant with another and the new regime was busy enclosing commons and raising taxes, Winstanley put his newly conceived radicalism into practice. Gathering like-minded people around him, Winstanley and his Diggers dug up common land on St George's Hill "to sow Corn, and to eat our bread together by the sweat of our brows".

The Digger movement expanded rapidly, inspiring the creation of communes in seven other counties. Although they were crushed by Cromwell's forces within a year, their legacy lived on in the radical undercurrents of a wide array of non-conformist sects and churches that flourished over the next century and a half. It was not until the aftermath of the French Revolution of 1789, however, that Winstanley's central focus on the ownership and use of land became prominent once more.

While the majority of the proto-socialist agitators who surfaced after 1789 concerned themselves with demands for universal male suffrage, and the radical religious groups became bewitched by millennial visions of an impending Apocalypse, three figures in particular turned their attention to radical agrarianism during the revolutionary upheaval that continued throughout the first half of the nineteenth century.

The first was Thomas Spence (1750-1814), who proposed that "private ownership of the land was the root of all social evil", and who was inspired by the jubilee proposed in the *Book of Leviticus*, an institution taking place every fifty years whereby land was redistributed to ensure that all members of the community were provided for on an equal basis. Spence was raised in Newcastle by Scottish Calvinist parents, and conceived his ideas while working as a teacher, but it was after he moved to London, around 1787, that his ideas began to be disseminated widely. The millenarian enthusiasms of the time convinced him that the jubilee was imminent, and he became involved in the London Corresponding Society, the leading radical organization of the time, influencing others who, after his death, convened three huge demonstrations in Spa Fields in the winter of 1816 and 1817 as attempts to fulfil their mentor's concept of the jubilee.

Spence's ideas in turn inspired Robert Owen (1771-1858), a committed communitarian and philanthropist who put radical theories of land use into practice for the first time since Winstanley. Owen began his career as an industrialist, owning a cotton mill at New Lanark where he instigated a policy of worthy social reform. In his writings of the 1820s he advocated model communities based on a mixture of manufacturing and agriculture, but as he began to establish his own co-operative communities–"villages of co-operation", as he himself described them–the industrial component became increasingly less important, and by 1842 he was writing that Britain "must now become essentially agricultural".

Owen's influence cannot be overstated. He was the inspiration for the founding of dozens of working class co-operative associations across the country, and he and his followers were responsible for the establishment of over a dozen experimental communes between 1821 and 1847. Most were short-lived, lasting no more than a few years, and have come to be overlooked by most historians as failures, but in this crucial period in British history, before the ultimate triumph of industrialization was assured, they were clearly a last-ditch attempt by frustrated artisans, excluded from the march of progress, to maintain their own dignity and autonomy. Owen's own assertion, that he would be "very sorry ever to have a cotton factory again, for the substantial wealth of the world is only obtained from the land", remains a poignant tribute to his radical vision.

The third influential figure of the period was Feargus O'Connor, the leader of the Chartists, who were initially set up to demand universal male suffrage and reform of the astonishingly corrupt parliamentary system. Throughout the 1830s and early 1840s, the Chartists "tried all the political strategies in the repertoire of radicalism, from constitutional lobbying to alternative assemblies, general strikes and armed uprisings", before conceiving their Land Plan, unveiled in 1845, which was described by the historian Jeremy Burchardt as "the most impressive manifestation of working class commitment to radical agrarianism".

Over the next four years, 70,000 shareholders in the Chartist Land Cooperative Society raised over £100,000, which was used to acquire over 1,100 acres of land, beginning with Herringsgate near Watford (renamed O'Connorville). In all, nearly 300 cottages were built at five separate locations for supporters who wished to become independent smallholders, or "radical English peasants", as the historian Jan Marsh described them. Each successful applicant–from what was essentially a high-minded lottery system–received between two and four acres of land, and although the scheme collapsed in 1851, having failed to find a secure legal basis for its activities, it achieved some measure of success as an antidote to the failure of the Chartists' wider political ideals.

After the collapse of the Owenite communities and the failure of the Chartists to effect profound change by either violent or non-violent means, radical agrarianism went underground once more, although there was a brief resurgence in the 1890s, when the adoption of anarchism–derived from the writings of Kropotkin and Tolstoy–led to the creation of eight separate communities, among them the Clousden Hill Communist and Cooperative Colony in Newcastle, which ran from 1895-1900, with up to two dozen members keeping animals and growing vegetables which they sold to local Cooperatives and markets, and the Norton Colony, near Sheffield, which ran from 1896-1900, surviving by selling vegetables from door to door in the local villages. Although the Clousden Hill Colony disbanded "through disagreements which there was no machinery to resolve", according to Jan Marsh, the equally non-hierarchical Norton Colony, where "all business [was] discussed and work arranged over the communal breakfast table", only came to an end when the lease expired, and one of its members, Hugh Mapleton, went on to found a health food firm that is still in business today.

THE COMMUNE HAD NO LEADERS, MIXED BATHING AND A BLATANT DISREGARD FOR MONEY

The most radical venture of the time was the "free commune" established in 1898 at Whiteway in the Cotswolds near Stroud, which endured near-starvation in its early years, particularly as its naïve members were all too willing to share what little they had with the hordes of visitors who appeared each summer. In its pure form–with no leaders, "free union" couples, mixed public bathing and a blatant disregard for money–the commune only survived until 1901, but it endured as a loose association of several dozen farmers and artisans until the 1930s, keeping alive something of its original spirit.

The last great period of Utopian dreaming began in the 1960s and is still with us today, taking in concerns as wide-ranging as the spiritual quest of the founders of Scotland's Findhorn

Foundation (established in 1962) and the radical politics of the London squatting scene. A prominent player in London's counter-culture of the 1960s was Sid Rawle, later described as the "King of the Hippies", who gave the youthful squatting movement some historical ballast by establishing the Hyde Park Diggers. Rawle was inspired by the example of Gerrard Winstanley, and, from the United States, by the more contemporary example of the San Francisco Diggers, also inspired by Winstanley, who set up communes and ran celebrated free food kitchens at the many free festivals that took place in California's hippie heyday.

By 1970, John Lennon was so impressed by Sid Rawle's revolutionary rhetoric that he offered him custodianship of Dorinish Island–a small, uninhabited island off the coast of County Mayo that Lennon had bought in 1967–for use as a Digger commune, "for the common good". After a brief recruitment drive amongst the hippies of London, 25 adults and a baby duly set off for Dorinish, where they stayed for two years, growing their own vegetables, which they stored in specially dug hollows, and cadging lifts off the local oyster fishermen every fortnight or so for supplementary shopping trips to Westport on the mainland. There was a certain amount of conflict–in March 1971 the *Connaught Telegraph* declared, "After a year of seething anger, Westport has finally declared war on the 'Republic of Dorinish'" –but the commune finally closed down of its own volition the folowing year, when a fire destroyed the main tent used to store supplies.

Rawle had made sporadic visits to England throughout the duration of the commune. At the first great free festival in Glastonbury in June 1971, for example, free food had been provided by two groups –the wittily named Communal Knead, and Sid's Diggers, now known as the Digger Action Movement. On his return to London in the spring of 1972, he took the Diggers' message on from Dorinish and Glastonbury into the growing free festival scene. He was one of the main organizers of the Windsor Free Festival, which squatted the Queen's backyard every August from 1972 to 1974 (when it was crushed by Thames Valley Police) and became a prominent figure in the Stonehenge Free Festival, which occupied the fields opposite Stonehenge every June from 1974 to 1984 (until it too was suppressed with unprecedented violence at the Battle of the Beanfield in 1985).

For many involved in the free festivals, their ultimate aim was the creation of viable alternative settlements, a position that was outlined in the Albion Free State manifesto of 1974: "The dispossessed people of this country need Land–for diverse needs, permanent free festival sites, collectives, and cities of Life and Love, maybe one every fifty miles or so, manned and womaned by people freed from dead-end jobs and from slavery in factories mass-producing non-essential consumer items".

In reality, however, with land so hard to come by and opposition from the land-owning establishment as implacable as it was in Winstanley's day, the free festival circuit settled for the most part on a necessary compromise, in which communal ideals of alternative settlements became centred on a nomadic lifestyle instead, although Sid Rawle and various other luminaries of the scene also became involved, in 1976, in the establishment of Tipi Valley in south Wales, one of the most enduring alternative communities of recent times.

After 1985, even the mobile Utopias of the travellers and the free festival scene were suppressed, although their spirit resurfaced in the underground rave scene and in particular in the road protest movement of the 1990s, when the Dongas tribe, and countless other activists inspired by their example, occupied sacred landscapes–Twyford Down, Solsbury Hill and the woods around Newbury, for example–for months on end, building up an intimate relationship with the land and defending it with formidable passion and ingenuity.

The Dongas subsequently disappeared into the green lanes of England on a more or less permanent basis, but they inspired in particular a coalition of volunteers known as The Land Is Ours (TLIO), whose campaigns included two separate occupations of land near St George's Hill in Surrey, where Winstanley's Diggers had begun their short-lived but influential campaign in 1649, and the establishment of an eco-village on thirteen acres of derelict land in Wandsworth.

The occupations of St George's Hill, which took place in 1995 and 1999, were largely symbolic gestures of communal living and farming that were designed to stimulate publicity and debate. The first occupation, which was TLIO's first major outing, only lasted a week, but during that time 600 volunteers occupied a disused airfield and set-aside land and managed to raise a temporary village, dig gardens, perform a play and distribute information in the neighbouring towns. The media coverage was favourable, and in the opinion of the campaigning journalist George Monbiot they "succeeded in generating the first stirrings of a national debate about land". 300 activists returned on the 350th anniversary of Winstanley's occupation, raising a stone marker commemorating his achievements, and once more occupying a small corner of the hill. This second occupation, which took place under the glare of a high-profile media spotlight, lasted a month, but on both occasions the campaigners' evictions were resonant with irony: the injunctions that were used to remove them were raised by the inhabitants of a luxury housing development that now occupies most of the common land where Gerrard Winstanley first began his bold experiment at land reform.

Elsewhere, the struggle to establish permanent, low-impact alternative communities remains blighted by two prevailing factors–the price of land, and more particularly the planning regulations that are designed, for the most part, to frustrate those without large amounts of money and influence. The communities that have survived have only done so after protracted wrangling with the authorities, among them the enduring community in Tipi Valley, where the hundred or so inhabitants have been involved in various court actions with the authorities since 1984, and Tinker's Bubble, a forty acre area of woodland and orchards in Somerset, which was bought by a group of ten settlers in 1993, including Simon Fairlie of Chapter 7, the planning wing of This Land Is Ours. Living in yurts and a number of exquisite self-built wooden houses, the settlers produce much of their own organic food and have become self-sufficient in energy, fuel and water by banning the use of fossil fuels and mains electricity and undertaking all work manually, with the aid of a Shire Horse and a wood-driven steam engine. After six years of resistance from the local authorities, they were finally granted five years' temporary planning permission in 1999.

The most shocking contemporary example of the hypocrisy and bigotry that is endemic in the planning departments of all levels of government concerns a low-impact, ecologically-sound Roundhouse that was built by Tony Wrench in 1997 in the Brithdir Mawr community, situated in the Pembrokeshire Coast National Park near Fishguard.

Since its solar panels were spotted from the air in 1999 by a helicopter scouring the countryside for signs of illegal caravans, government officials and the bureaucrats of the National Park Authority have campaigned remorselessly to demolish the Roundhouse. By the start of 2004, Tony and his partner Jane Faith were preparing to give up the fight, but on the Bank Holiday weekend at the start of May several hundred supporters, including representatives of The Land Is Ours, Chapter 7 and the Tinker's Bubble community, staged a number of high-profile demonstrations, occupying the reconstructions of Iron Age roundhouses in the nearby hill-fort of Castell Henllys, demonstrating outside the offices of the Park Authority and squatting Tony's Roundhouse to prevent him taking it down. At the time of writing, the Park Authority is still refusing to back down, but the protestors have pledged to return if any further attempts are made to demolish the Roundhouse.

What makes the indignation of the regulators particularly unpalatable is its sheer hypocrisy. The Welsh Assembly, for example, is one of only two governments in the world committed by law to the promotion of sustainable development, offering £750,000 over the next three years to support sustainable projects, which it describes on its website as 'treating the earth as though we intended to stay'. For its part, the National Park Authority, while demonising Tony Wrench, has been happy enough to approve the creation of a 500 acre, multi-million pound leisure and sports village–including 340 log cabins–within the boundaries of the National Park, and the bigotry that underpins its stance was explicitly spelled out just a few months ago by its head of "development control", Catherine Milner. Defending her opposition the Roundhouse Milner said, "Before long you won't have any countryside left because these people will be building these things all over the place". The tone is clear: corporate money will buy you whatever you want, but small-scale idealism is still anathema to the powers-that-be.

REFERENCES

BOOKS:

Jeremy Burchardt, *Paradise Lost: Rural Idyll and Social Change Since 1800* (I.B. Tauris, 2002)

Jan Marsh, *Back to the Land: The Pastoral Impulse in Victorian England from 1880 to 1914* (Quartet, 1982)

Andy Worthington, *Stonehenge: Celebration and Subversion* (Alternative Albion, 2004)

WEBSITES:

Chapter 7: www.thelandisours/chapter7

George Monbiot: www.monbiot.com

The Diggers: www.bilderberg.org/land/diggers.htm

The Land Is Ours: www.tlio.org.uk

Tinker's Bubble: resurgence.gn.apc.org/issues/monbiot211.htm

Tipi Valley: www.thelandisours.org/pubs/pdfs/rsforum.pdf

Tony Wrench's Roundhouse: www.thatroundhouse.info

A Capitalist Paradise

PENNY RIMBAUD LOOKS NO FURTHER THAN THE END OF HIS NOSE. ILLUSTRATIONS BY GED WELLS

Of all the manifestations promoted in the Old Testament, monotheism has more than any wreaked a terrible vengeance. The journey from the Garden of Eden to the Nazi death camps was as abhorrent as it was inevitable; while it was Christ who dug the pits, it was his dissenting brothers who took the leap through time into them. Wonderland was never so real: a sea of tears.

When Moses descended from on high, tablet in hand, he was declaring war on the playful polytheism which might have made of the Garden a heaven on earth. If ever the serpent struck, it was in Moses' singularity of purpose: the Commandments were given and the tribes set out across the globe to spread their venomous message: "thou shalt not." Prosperity was to be the reward for virtue and, to ensure success for the virtuous, a single God would sit in judgement. But the ears of Pan were as deaf to such sombre tones as were his eyes blind to such stoney tomes. Monotheism was as arid as the desert from which

MONEY IS A FORM OF DAY-TO-DAY SLEIGHT OF HAND

it was crafted. If Abraham was to become "father of many nations", the script would have to be re-written... enter the fall guy.

Where the singular landscape of the desert had given form to the psychological construct of monotheism, the rich fertility of the northern lands called for a greater diversity. Christ, the chosen one, King of the Jews, was to be the prophet, but first the essential schism had to be cleft. He must die that he might live. Christ's trial and crucifiction (sic) made three of one. The Father, the Son and the Holy Ghost, a trinity more deadly than the nails which sealed it: "greater love hath no man." Three was a crowd, hardly polytheistic, but it would do for the time being; saints, martyrs and mystics could be introduced later. It was a cheap trick, but as his-story has proved, an effective one. Throughout Europe the desert storms blew, and pagans and polytheists alike bowed their heads to the darkened skies and there was no mercy.

George Bush stalks the White House corridors chanting his mantra, "freedom or fear?" His voice rebounds, echoes. "Freedom or fear? Freedom or fear? I am the light. Whoever follows me will never walk in darkness. Freedom or..." Shadows lurk at every twist and turn: they are his, imprinted on time. The doors slam, but there's no one behind them. He is alone, afraid. He stumbles blindly into Van Gogh's yellow chair. It splinters into a bed of thorns on the plush, red pile carpet of his intrigue.

In heralding a breakdown in the arts and sciences, the Renaissance challenged the dominant culture in monotheism. Most crucially, perspective was invented, isolating individuals in space, leaving them free to think their own thoughts: this way, that way or the other. By then the papacy had already lost the plot: saints, mystics and martyrs. On every front, diversity was gaining ground. The single God was under threat. Enter Martin Luther.

Acting unwittingly on the individual licence created through perspective, Luther sought to re-establish fundamental Judaic/Christian values. He succeeded by dropping a can of worms into the fertile soils of the Renaissance, creating a union which bore the sour fruits of the Reformation. In turn, those fruits bore seed: the seeds of capitalism.

George Bush awakes from a dream, confused that Lilith has played him so well, shamed my the still moist map of his journey. "Freedom or fear?" and then, remembering his calling, "I am the way. I know it won't be easy for me or my family, but God wants me to do it." And the towers of Babylon fell.

Under guidance from Judaic/Protestant overlords, the Industrial Revolution paved the way for the supremacy of capitalism. In the manufacture of matter void of the diverse forms of content (Warhol's soup cans being an heroic if failed attempt to reverse this process), the Masters were at last able to reflect their Maker. With the rise of technology, the circle was complete, and capitalism was ready to go global: one God, one Maker, one product. Abraham's blessing could at last become a reality.

COKE ~ THE AMERICAN SCREAM

It was in Ancient Judaea that the primacy of economic values had first been given voice, but it was the Protestants and Jews of Europe and later, and more notably, the Protestants and Jews of America, who made of that voice the threnody that it has now become: God is love is plutocracy. Jew and Protestant as one. Mammon knows no bonds: God is He and He alone is God.

It should be no surprise then that in exercising his absolute power Bush should mirror the omnipotence of that single God. It is the lie at the very core of Freudian personality, the I that is ego, the call of the desert, the slander of ancient Sinai, the thunderbolts of despair, jackboots on the rail track, a pall of black smoke, the crow of carrion. Himmelsweg: the schism.

Transportation to the Nazi death camps was provided by the Reichsbahn, the German State Railway. "Passengers" were each allotted a one-way, third-class ticket. Children under ten travelled free. "Group fares" were available for numbers greater than three hundred. Tickets were paid for by the German State.

Despite his staggering inability to guarantee efficient rail services, Richard Branson recently announced that Virgin will "send" tourists into space by 2008 fuelled on a combination of laughing gas and liquid rubber. At least they'll bounce back with smiles on their faces. Branson's "fortune" is estimated to be around £3 billion. Now that's what I call a real laugh. Ho, ho, ho.

Given the enormous importance placed on money, it is hard to come to terms with its essentially abstract nature: it's a form of day-to-day sleight of hand which, like a bearded God on high, we are fooled into believing as fact, or at least believing we believe as fact. How then have we come to attach so much value to it when clearly its worth is no more than the worth we attach to it? A wad of banknotes means nothing in itself, it requires us to invest it with value: the Mint may print it, but it's we who screen the meaning. It's the perfect paradox; a worthless piece of paper with an exclusively subjective value, which is, of course, why it's so hideously seductive. Like religion, we refuse to objectify it because if we did we would bring ourselves one step closer to the fundamental emptiness of our existence. Preferring the security of deceit, we choose to believe that, like the magician's rabbit, we weren't pulled from nowhere. In short, a trick well played is good enough for most of us, which is why we're so adept at playing tricks on ourselves. That'll be 10/6d.

The empire of chemical giant IG Farben, whose subsidiaries include Bayer, BASF, Agfa and Degesh (manufacturers of Zyklon B), was built on the emaciated corpses of slave labour, the very foundation of most corporations: wholly and unwholesomely global. To this day IG Farben have not been brought to account.

BE SURE, YOUR SINS WILL FIND YOU OUT

WHICH, AS IT IS YOU WHO HAS COMMITTED THEM, SEEMS TO POSE LITTLE PROBLEM

Orwell's 1984. Kerbang. Bhopal's Big Brother, Union Carbide pesticide plant, plants a nasty on local inhabitants. Methyl isocyanate kills thousands and leaves quarter of a million suffering exposure-linked diseases. To avoid worldwide boycott, Union Carbide sells on to the makers of Agent Orange, Dow Chemicals

(apocalypse now) and Bayer (holocaust then). Now and then the clouds drift by, but ostriches need no umbrella.

One man's pound is worth another man's twenty: modern-day alchemy. What's five-score actually worth? Ten awful paperback novels or an awful lot of tabloids, twenty bottles of average wine or one average meal for two plus wine, ten or so hand-jobs down a piss-stinking back alley or one in a crummy massage parlour. Who's paying who for what, and why is the White Rabbit always late?

BASF manufacture vitamins. They're good for y/our w/health.

Money is the meanest form of energy. It undermines our natural creative processes, denies us our nomadic rights and divorces us from the cornucopia of life's native gifts, hedgerow vitamins being amongst them. Giving unto Ceasar was a ten per cent investment for the future: an insurance policy which didn't seem to work too well for Christ. No one ever seems to mention the other ninety per cent. Is it any wonder then that the planet's two meanest religions, Judaism and

Protestantism, should be so central to the growth of capitalism? When the Jews were the lenders, the Gentiles were the borrowers. So who colluded with whom? Who were the usurers? It's better understood as a construct. When the temple tables were turned, the cash fell into the same hands. The single God was and is the usurer.

HOW ARE WE TO METER REWARD EXCEPT THROUGH ITS MONETARY WORTH?

JAN 1889
NIETZSCHE COLLAPSES UNDER OWN WEIGHT

Having failed to heed Friedrich's dramatic warning, not only do we continue to suffer the dual intellectual gags of Judaic/Protestant ideology. But also their physical manifestation in gross materialism: one God, one Mammon. Where the Catholic has the outlet of the confessional, "forgive me, Father", the Protestant and the Jew have no way out. It is their burden to prove their worth in this life that their sins may be atoned come the Day of Judgement. But how are we, let alone God, to meter worth except by reward, and how are we to meter reward except through its monetary worth? In this context the Lottery is a form of sacrament, the winners being guaranteed one-way access to the Kingdom of Heaven, that being the one reigned over by God, Queen and the Chief Rabbi, and never mind the mortgage. Heavens above, earthly goods are not purchased for earthly prize: the mythical Joneses are a metaphor for God. When we depart this mortal coil we can't take our wealth with us, so how else is God to know our value but through its manifestation in earthly form? Eyes in the back for the head? Tell that to the army chaplain. Rolex? Bollox, it's just a timepiece for eternity, within Judaic/Protestant ideology it's a passport into it. In short, the message is singular; capitalism is quite literally God-sent.

Having been thus commodified within the framework of God the Father's monovision doctrine, it is only natural, indeed righteous, that we should then gladly allow ourselves to be used, and if need be exterminated, by those elders who actually "know" the spiritual value of money: "to know him is to love him". In this manner, through being no more than the commodity that we are, our energies are transmuted into money which we can then exchange for commodities, the best of which taking the abstract form of solid investments, which are, naturally, no more solid than air. Now you see me, now you don't. Within this construct we become indistinguishable from the commodities we purchase. We are, in fact, what we buy. Faustian to the end, we buy ourselves because we've sold ourselves. We are both indivisible and invisible.

We are born that we might die; a heavenly circle which in fact knows no death nor, indeed, life, but we're sold the line and we buy the line. The ultimate self-sacrifice: no self at all. We are Christ the Jew on the cross: the one and the same. Good Protestants are good Jews, obsessed with a concept of both spiritual and physical auto-destruct, that they too might die for their own sins. Hell, no one needs to hang around (metaphorically speaking) when they see their executioners

"I'M ONLY DOING MY JOB," MEANS: "I PUT MONEY BEFORE MORALITY"

appear over the hilltop. Gethsemane? It makes slavery seem positively benign. The good Jew is the good Protestant. "Eli, Eli, lema sabachthani."

If time was money, which, unless you own a Rolex, it isn't, there'd be forty-eight hour days. Shocking? Well, as it is we've got twenty-four-hour ones, so who's measuring what with what? In the time it takes multi-billionaire Donald Trump to flick back his brush-over and slip a sweaty paw into current wife Melania's blouse, he's probably earned a thousand times more than the year's wages paid to the poor devil who dug out the diamonds adorning the crucifix hanging in the valley-shadows of her cleavage.

Those who, we are told, don't understand the value of money (largely those who do not fit into the Judaic/Protestant fold) are those who conveniently will never be offered a practical lesson in its use. The only real investment made by capitalism in those outside the fold is in their destruction. Genocide, as Hitler was honest enough to bring to public notice, is a central part of the agenda. It's an agenda which preceded the Nazis in the days of Empire, and continues unabated to this very moment led by World Powers: the corporations, the international banks and the World Traders in their now cerebral towers. In repeatedly claiming that the Holocaust was "man's darkest hour", the World Powers have created a convenient smokescreen beneath which they may enthusiastically pursue their own programmes of death. That Nazi policies of 'lebensraum" have been so actively employed against the Palestinians by the Israeli State is proof enough that within the capitalist framework the pot is every bit as black as the kettle.

VENGEANCE IS MINE, SAITH THE LORD

The eradication of human detritus, "undesirables", knows no boundaries. From the plains of America to the deserts of Africa, Mammon has wielded his sword. To the capitalist overlords, we are all inhabitants of Ground Zero and, if by chance we aren't, we can very quickly be made so. Lest we forget, globalisation is no more than a cosy euphemism: death's the game, death's the name. The desert storms of Judaic/Protestant thought are more powerful today than they have ever been. In the Great Holocaust of time, regardless of race or creed, we are no more than pawns. In our age of treason, the key hitmen are comfortable seated behind the polished oak desks of the White House and Number Ten, their fingers on the button.

WAITING ON THE BORDERLINES OF TIME

Existentially, the eradication of debt in Africa will prove to be the eradication of Africa and its people: it's an SAP, a sop. And if Africa cannot be "liberated" existentially (which it will not be), then, like Iraq, it will be bombed into submission. That's the real meaning of money.

A tribesman stands one-footed on the brow of the escarpment, his earth-coloured, earth-covered cloak blowing out like a battle flag in the warm

Sahara wind, his spear pointing to the heavens of which he knows nothing. The double-forked lightning of time strikes, and the tribesman is no more.

Melania likes her crucifix. She may be a Catholic, but so what? She's a woman, and that's worse. The crucifix is platinum, thirty-two rocks. Donald likes Melania regardless of her religion, and despite her being a woman. It was he who bought the crucifix. Donald likes tits, they're his needle's eye. There's no stopping him. Platinum, thirty-two rocks and a string of pearls: gotcha.

Cash or crucifix, either way they'll get you in the end, and when they've finished with you, they'll find another. There's always another.

AUSCHWITZ ~ A LONG WAY FROM THE MOON. SCOOP.

WERNER VON BRAUN'S GIANT STEP FOR MANKIND

The "Einsatzgruppen", Nazi murder squads, were made up from the élite of the German professional middle class. They were jolly decent people, just like you and me.

Money is a justification, an inverted morality. Professionalism is the antithesis of authenticity. "I'm only doing my job," means "I put money before morality," Empty lime into the cattle-trucks, pull the trigger on an unarmed eleven-year-old Iraqi, release the bolt through a cow's head, all actions which readily fit into the Judaic/Protestant framework. Call it meat. Call it freedom. Call it democracy. Write your restaurant reviews for your rapacious readership, pump out your porn for the parasites, shackle yourself to credit-controlled wage slavery. You're only doing your job. But whose job? If you're "doing" a job, it's not yours, it's somebody else's, someone who is getting rich on your stupidity. Stupidity? OK, need for security. Security? Well, a dumbed-down sense of insecurity. Insecurity? Blame Murdoch and his minions and then get stuck into your Weekend Guardian. It's more than the week's end, but you won't know that 'til you get a life. So forget the millions and call it religion. Accept that Murdoch's as close to God as you're ever gonna get. Now look at the schisms.

FIVE DEAD IN CARAVAN FIRE

Sod the IMF, there's nothing funny about money, no zen in the yen nor scruple in rouble. It's not money, but fear which is the dominant currency of capitalism, its spirituality. "It could happen again": the very core of the Judaic/Protestant ethos. It could happen again because "again" still exists deep within our warped psychology. Freud saw to that.

Where Nietzsche by executing the One might have freed the many, Freud, a good Judaic/Protestant boy if ever there was one, single-mindedly slid into the twentieth century, hammer in hand, to nail the single God to the awry cross of id. From now on there was no escape. Our deepest inner soul had been commodified and God was back in the marketplace.

Salvation? You are what you buy. Gadgets, gewgaws, trinkets, trash: the cluster bombs of consumerism. For or against? You buy what you are. In a world every-stripped of its diversity, WTC is the new XTC, a meaning within the emptiness of techno-capitalism, a cathode-ray fix, the latest high in an all-time low. But remember this in your drooling sentimentality, the WTC wasn't a holocaust it was a Reichstag.

IT WILL HAPPEN AGAIN

Special Weapons Observation Reconnaissance Detection Systems, SWORDS (robot killing machines with more intelligence than your average grunt), are being developed on your taxes by Blair's Ministry Of Defence for the benefit of the Bush-associated Carlyle Group (www.carlyle.com). Action Man is coming alive while shareholders rub their hands in glee. Call it just another hand-job. Meanwhile, scientists at the University of California (universities having once been known as "seats of learning") are grafting the living tissue of rats onto robotic skeletons in the hope that the results will give an acceptably "lifelike" appearance.

SUPER FANTASY VINYL DOLLY BUSTER. SHE'S NAUGHTY. SHE'S NICE. SHE VIBRATES. SHE HAS THREE HOLES [TWO MORE THAN THE AVERAGE]. SHE'S YOUR S FOR THE TAKING. ALL CARDS ACCEPTED.

BARBYS, Basic Active Replica Bridal Yoke Systems, are currently being developed at the University of Pittsburgh. Not only will they act as Action Man's partner, they'll become an absolute must for all us discerning gents: tight as a rat's arse. American Express? Plastic money in the cyber-brothel of American bankruptcy.

Kerbang, the broker takes a toke and future the only future he'll look to is in futures: transparent to the point of non-existence. Alice dives through the looking-glass. Don't look back. The Emperor wears no clothes because the Emperor has no body on which to wear them. Enter the SWORDS. They're killers, and they can't see their own reflection. Alice swims away in a sea of mucus. A bearded freak takes out a matchbox to light up his toecap. Nice shoes, nice try, but he's got no interest in interest and that, like it or not, is his real crime. Kerbang.

SIX HUNDRED CARAVANS OR ONE WTC? EXCLUSIVE

THE THEORY OF RELATIVITY IN A BOMBSHELL.

It's a fact. It's a Donna Karan in white, all thru the night. It's a Ralph Lauren in red: red on the bed. It's trump and true, dollar hard, popping the blue. Stars and stripes and Kleenex wipes: BARBYS.

Money is sex. Money is power. Money is surrogate. Money is monotheistic. We're all Jews. Christ was merely a schism: two sides to a two-faced coin. We're all Protestants. Magdalene was the mother of whores. We're all prostitutes.

BASRA OBLITERATED. PICTURES

JUST ANOTHER BIG APPLE IN ANOTHER BIG GARDEN

WASPS IN GARDEN ATTACK

....

As those tragic towers toppled to the homicidal connivance of the modern-day American State (that which was founded on SS intelligence and Jewish money), liquid assets oozed like black gold from its vaults, ran in dark streams from its marbled emporiums, past helpless security guards disarmed in their confusion, and out onto the cinder-baked streets. Tossing aside the theatre of sorrow, reptilian shoals of cocaine-driven brokers, Prozac-popping investors and

Valium-blind shareholders rushed forward to consider possible gain through the consolidation of impossible loss; shipless pirates training their singular eyes upon a singular windfall: Ground Zero. A modern-day crucifixion. Who really questioned from whence the storm had blown? Three thousand martyrs for the cause of oil. Who really cared? Yet even before that burnt offering to Mammon, the terrible vengeance that could be wrought in its name has been contrived by those who breathed the noxious breath of intrigue. Democracy's whores were free at last to unleash the ghoul of hegemony that for so long they had been nurturing: a war that will last a lifetime-Afghanistan, Iraq, Iran, Syria, North Korea: the list is endless, the message is clear. But Lord, dear Lord, how many lifetimes do we have? And as the planet is bludgeoned into cowering submission, and innocents are slaughtered in their thousands, corpulent corporate tycoons will be aided form the clammy leather back-seats of over-stretched limos to be led to illicit private bookings. They'll puff on cigars big as their biggest phallic fantasies, salivate over very special menus, feed their dyspepsia and belch, rank on usury while speculating on the rise and fall of their pubescent escorts' cleavages and the rock-solid investments that hang between them. Oh yes, diamonds are a girl's best friend, but a wife's worst enemy. Sated by excess, and an obsession with possession which now threatens to smother even their innate ignorance, the tired tycoons will clench their fat arses and reach out their porky hands towards their torpid escorts' powdered flesh, seeking to leech from it a life-blood that in all their crumpled decadence they have never known. And in the pitiful self-delusion of this hedonistic hell, the neon will flash and the billboards bray, and through the damnable pall of war the catch-phrase will remain the same: "if you're not with us, you're against us–consume." And in their self-imposed impotence, the crowds will be eager to oblige. The old world of cheese-cake security has been unceremoniously binned, but the new world will be gift-wrapped. Money changes hands, but always ends up in the same pockets. Friend or foe, what does it matter? You only live once; that much now seems painfully conclusive. The essence is simple, Ground Zero is the post-modernist symbol of capitalism, the heart and soul, the sordid justification. There's no option now but to dive deeper into the belly of the ravaged beats. Don't think: buy. Don't stop: spend. Prove to yourself that you still exist. Consume or be consumed. Ciao, bambino. Buy, buy.

....

FUKUYAMA'S CAPITALIST PARADISE AS THE END OF HISTORY?
FUCK YOU, FRANCIS

Time is Funny

JAY GRIFFITHS REBELS AGAINST THE NOTION OF TIME AS FIXED, REGULAR AND MONOTONE. PHOTOGRAPHY BY CHRIS DRAPER

Clocks: caging time. The watch: the manacle on the wrist. Deadlines like barbed wire. Coercive, cruel, crushing speed. Punctuality next to godliness. The work ethic. Efficiency *über alles*. Western Christian time, linear, dry, masculine and ripped away from nature, exemplified in the clock, tediously ticking you off, count, count, count.

By contrast, picture this. A gibbet, a drawbridge, flags, turrets and oil drums. Made of scrap metal, wit and anarchy; place of white cider and Attitude. Welcome to Fort Trollheim, built by eco-activists who lived in their Fort, and up in treehouses in the nearby trees, opposing a road in Devon, in the mid 1990s. And they had their manifesto: "This is the Independent Free State of Trollheim... we have no allegiance to the UK government... We do not recognize history, patriarchy, matriarchy, politics, communists, fascists or lollipop men/ladies... We have a hierarchy based on dog worship... Our currency is to be based on the quag barter system. We do not recognize the Gregorian calendar: by doing so this day shall be known as One... Be afraid, be afraid, all ye that hear. Respect this State."

Time is a political subject. It is a crucial part of the language of power, between nations, and classes, between men and women, between humankind and nature. Stealthily, nastily, one type of time has grown horribly dominant: clock-dominated, work-oriented, coercive, capitalist and anti-natural: Hegemonic Time.

The Benedictine monasteries first began scheduling time, controlling and ordering time according to Christian dictat. With the sixth century Rule of Saint Benedict, idleness, that impish spirit, was decreed "the enemy of the soul". Crucially, bells would be rung not only through the day but through the night too, for the night was the time when even the most well-behaved monks could slope off, free in their dream times. By ringing bells through the day, the monasteries commanded the bodies of the monks; by ringing bells through the night, the order of Christian time would get into their very minds.

The Industrial Revolution radically altered the sense of time experienced by the common people, and it created time-owners; the capitalist factory-owners, erecting clock-bound fences of work-time and the sense that employers owned the time of their employees, enslaving their time, enclosing time. This time, and all the time-values which go with it, has been imposed on numerous cultures across the world in a widespread and unacknowledged piece of cultural imperialism.

What's the time? Dishonest question. A political question. There are thousands of times, not one. But this one mono-time has worldwide dominance. Greenwich Mean Time comes reeking with the language of imperialism and smug with the knowledge that time is power: the chief clock at Greenwich in 1852 was called the "master" clock; it sent out signals to "slave" clocks at London Bridge. All the history of time-keeping and the discovery of longitude enabled Britons to rule the oceans and then build its empires of land. Having built its empires of land, it set about building empires of time, enslaving people's lives and enclosing other cultures' times with the One Hegemonic Time. When missionaries arrived amongst the Algonquin people of North America, the Algonquin, outraged, called clock-time "Captain Clock" because it seemed to command every act for the Christians.

Time has always been allied to power, for revolutionaries, rulers or reactionaries. Calendars and clocks have always been an ideological, political and religious weapon. Potentates, princes and priests, hypnotized by hopes of hegemony, have always stood on the borders of space and looked at time–for time is a kingdom, a power and a glory.

Pol Pot declared 1975 to be "Year Zero", marking the beginning of his rule as if it were the beginning of time itself. The Third Reich was to last a thousand years. When the ancient Chinese empire had colonized some new region, the phrase they used was both sinister and telling; the new territory had "received the calendar". In a phrase which I also find very sinister, the ultra-right wing, in power in the USA today, have their project for global domination named by Time: the Project for the New American Century.

In 1370, Charles V of France gave an order that all clocks were to be set by the magnificent clock in his palace; he was the ruler of lands and now would be ruler of time. But wherever there are clock rulers, there are clock rebels, and in the French Revolution, Charles V's clock was severely damaged in an act of articulate vandalism. A new time-measurement was announced: 1792 made Year One.

Speed is intimately tied to power. It is an index to status, so waiters, those who wait, putting their time on hold for others, are low-status, low-earning. VIPs, whose time is considered valuable, must never be kept waiting. The entire transport system, from Concorde to a Mercedes to high speed trains, is set up to serve the rich, to serve them fastest. (Oh, what transports of élites.) Italian Futurists wanted to straighten out the Danube so that it would flow faster; the natural rivers of time literally made to run for human speed. There is a nasty, steely connection between speed and fascism. Italian Futurist Marinetti glorified speed and supported fascism. Nazis put money into land speed record attempts and Hitler began a huge road-building project (propaganda films being entitled *Fast Roads* and *Roads Make Happiness*).

By contrast, if you look at the notes on politically subversive singer Manu Chao's CD *Esperanza* it says: "This CD was born of much work, many journeys, spliffs and meetings. It was born without hurry, (because speed kills)." Westernized cultures think speed is automatically "good". This is not a universal understanding: to some people speed is immoral. To the Kabyle people of Algeria, speed is considered both indecorous and demonically over-competitive. (The Kabyle refer to the clock as the "devil's mill".)

Where there is Hegemonic Time, there is also subversive time, best represented in carnival, play, the cyclical nature of women, all children, and the cultures across the world who (just about) remember their own sense of time. For every ruler, there has been a rebel, for every power-hungry politician, there has been a carnivalesque protester, for every man too keen on imposing his white, linear calendar, there has been a woman who cyclically bleeds all over it.

Subversive and mischievous, carnival reverses the norms, overturns the usual hierarchies. Unlike Dominant Hegemonic Time, carnival is tied to nature's time; linked to cyclic, frequently seasonal events. Carnival transforms work-time to play-time, up-ends power structures and reverses the *status quo*. It is frequently earthy and sexual. Carnival is vulgar: of the common people. And it

TIME HAS ALWAYS BEEN ALLIED TO POWER, FOR REVOLUTIONARIES, RULERS, OR REACTIONARIES

is vulgar in another sense: drunken, licentious, loud and lewd.

Few festivals are more flamboyantly vulgar than May Day, or Beltane. This was one pagan festival which the disapproving Christian church did not – could not – colonise; it kept its raw smell of sexual licence and its populist grassroots appeal – which was why it was such a natural choice for the socialist movement. Vicarless and knickerless, traditionally lads and lasses went into the forests and woods to get a tree for the Maypole and so doing let rip the glorious fornications of May (May sex led to June weddings – June was the commonest month for marriages, with the full moon of June called the "mead" moon – the "honey" moon.) The May Day "Green Man" or Jack in the Green, dressed in leaves, carried a huge horn ('nuff said). The Maypole, the phallic pole planted in "mother" earth was the key symbol of this erotic day.

Then came the Puritans,

> "THE DEADLY STATISTICAL CLOCK, WHICH MEASURED EVERY SECOND WITH A BEAT LIKE A RAP UPON A COFFIN LID"

sniffing the rank sexuality and decrying the maypole as "this stinking idol" and in 1644 the Puritans banned Maypoles. In the nineteenth century, Victorians bowdlerised and infantilised May Day, making it a child's festival to emphasise innocence. Indeed.

Carnival emphasizes commonality; customs of common time celebrated by common people on common land. In Britain, a huge number of these customs disappeared as a result of one thing: enclosures, for when rights to common land were lost, so were the common carnivals. And just as land was literally fenced off – enclosed – so the spirit of carnival – broad, unfettered unbounded exuberance – was metaphorically enclosed.

Around the world, Christian missionaries outlawed carnivals and festivities of other cultures; Native American potlatches banned. Australian Aboriginal corroborees banned. South American traditional dances and festivals banned.

But carnival erupts, even today, the deliberate use of carnivalesque costume amongst anti-globalization protesters today, CIRCA, the Clandestine Insurgent Rebel Clown Army, seriously playing out the politics of carnival.

One thing which Dominant, Hegemonic Time has insisted on, is the importance of harnessing peoples' time for work; Time is Money, they say, without quite answering whose money is made out of whose time. When the Industrial Revolution rolled in, it chucked thousands of people into factories working for absurdly long hours. But there was protest. Workers in Britain, in the 1820s and 1830s smashed the clocks above the factory gates in protest at the theft of their time. Trade Unions took on first the abuse of time, seeking shorter working hours. Karl Marx highlighted the exploitation of workers' time in capitalism. Dickens wrote *Hard Times*, his blistering portrait of factory time and its deadening character: the "deadly statistical clock which measured every second with a beat like a rap upon a coffin lid." British workers staunchly persisted in honouring 'Saint Monday' and French workers "Saint-Lundi" (in effect the patron saint of hangovers). Protest continued, from the 1960s revolt against work, the refusal to wear watches, the slogan "Work less, Live more!" and today's "Downshifters" and assiduous Idlers.

So let us Play. Play has long been opposed to the work-dominated Western time. Play, that subversive beastie, anarchic, energetic and creative, is still hated by modern day Puritans of corporate capitalism, overworking its employees. All over the world, colonization included insistence on work time: Columbus, on first meeting the Tainos people (San Salvador) was convinced the people should be "made to work, sow and do all that is necessary and to adopt our ways..." The Inuit refer to themselves as "rich in knowledge, meat and time" and anthropologists have referred to hunter-gatherers as "the original affluent society" in that the pleasures and necessities of life could be

STRAND
LONDON.

ONE OF THE MOST TENACIOUS CONCEPTUAL THREATS TO WORK AND TIME IS CHILDHOOD ITSELF

secured with a minimum of work. Traditionally, many indigenous peoples do not have a designated word for work, and do not work for more than four hours a day; the length of time Bertrand Russell suggested in "In Praise of Idleness", reducing both overemployment and underemployment. He also argues that "there is far too much work done in the world, that immense harm is caused by the belief that work is virtuous." Leisure, by contrast, is "essential to civilisation".

The play ethic is far more, well, ethical than the work ethic. Play is freedom, is creation, is energy, is wicked flirtatiousness, is the helplessly laughing, the leglessly laddered, the god of Things which Brimmeth Over, the pint down the pub, the de trop overflow of excess, the resplendently unnecessary and the one-too-many which make the whole damn thing worthwhile. Play is harvest, is abundance, is generosity, the harvest of pleasure after work, the excess and the gusto, the more-than-enough, the gifts, the spirit of exchange. Take the word "giggling". A one-word harvest of play's superfluity, its liquid, lovely over-indulgence, it has g's to spare, (g, the funniest consonant. You want proof? Gnu. Gneed I say more?) and it fills the gaps with "i"–the quickest, wittiest, lickspittiest, trippiest and lightesthearted of all the vowels.

One of the most tenacious conceptual threats to work, and to Captain Clock's Hegemonic Time, is childhood itself. Children have a dogged, delicious disrespect for work-time, punctuality, efficiency and for schooled uniform time. Their time is an eternal-present. They live (given half a chance) pre-industrially, in tutti-frutti time, roundabout time, playtime; staunch defenders of the ludic revolution, their hours are stretchy, ribboned, enchanted and wild: which is why adults want to tame their time so ferociously, making them clock-trained, teaching them conventions of time-measurement as if they were concrete fact. The school clock is pointed to as the ultimate authority which even the Head obeys.

The exterior public clock and calendar of Hegemonic Time is white, clean, regular, predictable, objective, linear, homogenous and male. I'm not. No woman is. It's in the blood, the inner, personal, idiosyncratic, cyclical time; red, staining. When I'm ovulating, I'm not the same as when I'm premenstrual. At one pole I may well be cooperative, relaxed and nice. A good time to fill in forms and be polite. At the other, I play with fire and know my wildest most feral emotions. I will be intense, difficult, powerful and unpredictable. (Probably.) Pliny the Elder wrote of menstruating women: "Hardly can there be found a thing more monstrous than is that flux and course of theirs." Well, no. It's more majestic than monstrous, more mysterious than disgusting and its burning, volcanic energy is more immense than Pliny ever knew. That Pliny died because of just such a burning volcano gives me a certain mischievous pleasure. (But only when I'm premenstrual.)

Menstruation gives women an experience of time which inherently subverts Hegemonic Time. It is a critical, cuspish catch of time, time coloured and fluxy, flukey. Masculine society seeks to deny or penalize this time, to mock or scorn or (at best) ignore it. But this is when many women find their power, veering off at a subversive angle from the objective, public line of time. Menstrual absenteeism, deplored by many employers, is rightly relished by many women, for these days are quintessentially her own and do not belong to another. Weird and exceptional, her time of the month is radically opposed to uniform straight-line neat time.

Patriarchy hates flows–the literal flow of menstruation most viscerally, but hates all things which femalely flow, and does so with moral fervour. What is "perfect" is unflowing, unchangeable, eternal and male. Aristotle thought the male body perfect and the female imperfect. Leonardo da Vinci used the male body to show its supposed mathematical perfection. Aristotle also thought the heavens eternal and male and the earth changeful and female; the superior/inferior statuses not lost on the Christian church. Said Virgil: Women are ever things of many changing moods.

Changelessness is privileged over changefulness. Jesus Christ, like suburbia, the same yesterday, today and forever. I'm not. We're not. We're bloody well changing all the bloody time.

Our time is different. All our times are different. How many months are there in a year? Twelve according to the male public calendar, thirteen moon months, though, for women. The word for menstruation in so many languages is connected to words for moon. The moon, worldwide, represents women, female time and female deities while the sun gods are male. Moreover the characteristics of the sun and moon, nature's greatest time pieces, are attributed to men and to women respectively and given very different status. The sun does not change, whereas the moon changes completely, from full to new. The changeful attributes accorded to women have negative connotations; we are capricious, fickle, chancy; Lady Luck, we are notorious for changing our minds. Above all, we are cyclical, we turn and turn, we are time changing and returning, and herein is, to me, one of the key aspects of the sexual politics of time; it underlines everything, from the washing up to the triumph of patriarchal religions.

Let's start with the charladies. (The char in "charlady" is from Anglo Saxon word meaning "to turn"; repetitive cyclical and low status "chores" are for women.)

"Few tasks are more like the torture of Sisyphus than housework, with its endless repetition: the clean becomes soiled, the soiled is made clean, over and over, day after day," Simone de Beauvoir commented. Or: "I hate housework! You make the beds, you do the dishes–and six months later you have to start all over again" as Joan Rivers put it. Traditional women's work is cyclic, it must be done over and over again. and it reveals a genderised attitude to time; what is cyclical, though it keeps life itself flowing, is devalued.

Leave the washing up for a further horizon. For hunter-gatherers or early agricultural peoples, Time was seen as cyclical, moving in the seasons of the year, visible in the cycles of the moon. This idea of Time as a cycle is by far the commonest shape. The Native American Hopi people pictured time as a wheel. In Hindu thought, time moves in the unimaginably long cycles of the Kalpas. The modern western view of time, however, is linear, and one expert on the philosophy of time says this is highly unusual, "one of the peculiar characteristics of the modern world."

The image of linear time was forged by the great patriarchal religions, in particular Judaeo-Christianity. St Augustine argued that the history of the universe is "single, irreversible, rectilinear". Rebirth or reincarnation, with its implied cyclic time, was overruled by the linear descent of father-son genealogies (Salma begat Boaz and Boaz begat Obed and Obed begat Jesse.)

This is the nub of it: religions that saw time as linear–phallic in shape–were those that were patriarchal–phallic in character. Ever since, time has been organised on male lines, rather than in female cycle.

The Alcherringa or Dreamtime of Aboriginal Australians is perhaps the most extraordinary of all ideas of time. The Dreamtime looks at first sight like "the past" but it isn't. Subtle, ambiguous and diffuse, the Dreamtime is past, present and future merged, the Aboriginal "now" porous to the Dreamtime "forever"–the past and the future are membranes surrounding the present.

In the Western view, the past can be discussed as an abstraction. All over the world, indigenous peoples see the past as inextricably identified with–and embedded in–the land. The Harakmbut people in the Peruvian Amazon say, "Without the knowledge of history, the land has no meaning and without the land neither the Harakmbut history nor the culture has any meaning." In Australia, the Aboriginal Ancestors "live" in spite of death: they disappeared, but did not die. They did not "become nothing" but "became the country". The past is immanent in the land. "History," says Aboriginal Australian writer Herb Wharton, "comes up from the land."

Perhaps the most chasmic difference between the two is that the Western view sees the past as "dead", while the indigenous view sees the past as profoundly "alive". The land is animated with the past, and the past still exists–a different modality of time and one which has a reciprocal relationship with the present. Singing the stories of the Ancestors of the Dreamtime is not memory of time past, but participation in a diffuse, metaphoric depth of time-present. The Dreamtime sustains the present through "djang", the spiritual energy in the land, while the present, in turn, sustains the Dreamtime through myth and ritual. The indigenous view of the past, then, is different from the western in representation, in shape, character, significance and in vitality. But there's more. The inherently differing notions of the past have direct–and contemporary–political consequences. If the underground past is a source of sacred energy to indigenous people, it is merely a source of literal energy, fuel, to the western mind. Mining companies devastate indigenous land all over the world.

Gutenberg's printing press printed calendars before bibles; Hegemonic Time was mass-produced to go global. In one of the most pernicious lies in history, the Christian calendar and the clock of capitalism insisted that they represented time itself. The Christian calendar, (abstract, numerical and inherently political) has been used to deny the plurality of calendars across the world. Time itself, sensuous, poetic and diverse, is not found in it.

Amongst many peoples, "Time" is a matter of timing. It involves spontaneity rather than scheduling, sensitivity to a quality of time. Unclockable. The San Bushmen of the Kalahari do not plan when to hunt, but rather "wait for the moment to be lucky", reading and assessing animal patterns, looking for the "right" time. Timing for many indigenous peoples, for example, the Ilongot of the Philippines, is variable and indeterminate and unpredictable. Time is a subtle element where creativity and improvisation, flexibility, fluidity and responsiveness can flourish. People's responses to timing issues are subtle and graceful. But the dominant culture, far from respecting these socially graceful ideas of time, chooses to refer disparagingly to "Mexican time," "Maori time", "Indian time."

What subverts the dead hand of the dominant clock? Life itself. The elastic, chancy, sensitive times chosen for hunting depend on living things: how the living moment smells. There is a "biodiversity of time" imaged in cultures around the world, time as a lived process of nature. There is a scent-calendar in the Andaman forests, star-diaries for the Kiwi peoples of New Guinea and Aboriginal Australians who begin the cultivation season when the Pleiades appear. In Rajasthan a moment of evening is called "cattle-dust time", the Native American Lakota people have the "Moon of the Snowblind". One indigenous tribe in Madagascar refers to a moment as "in the frying of a locust". The English language still remembers time intrinsically connected to nature, doing something "in two shakes of a lamb's tail" or the (arbitrary and sadly obsolete) phrase "pissing-while".

For nature shimmers with time; and interestingly, many areas rich in myth and indigenous history are shown to be places of high biodiversity; living history, life at its liveliest. Both past and present equally vivacious, in a vital land.

The clock is not a synonym for time. It is, if anything, the opposite of time. The leaders of the Zapatistas insisted their time was not the time of the Westernized Mexican government. The Zapatistas took their orders from the peasants, and this was a very slow and unschedulable process. "We use time, not the clock. That is what the government doesn't understand." Subcomandante Marcos, in March 2001 in Mexico City spoke to thousands: "Tlahuica. We walk time... Zoque. We carry much time in our hands. Raramuri. Here the dark light, time and feeling."

> WHAT SUBVERTS THE DEAD HAND OF THE DOMINANT CLOCK? LIFE ITSELF

For time is not found in dead clocks and inert calendars, time is not money but is life itself: in ocean tides and the blood in the womb, in every self-respecting player, in the land, in every spirited protest for diversity and every refusal to let another enslave your time, in the effervescent gusto of carnival; life revelling in rebellion against the clock.

Jay Griffiths is the author of Pip Pip: A Sideways Look at Time *(Flamingo, £12.99)*

R

Ladders of Hope

Simon Busch heralds a new squatting boom. Illustrations by Nicky Deeley

Regardless of whether you will ever get a foot on the so-called property ladder it is assumed, at least, that you want to. But there is a group of people, their voices drowned out in the babble of home-owning hysteria, for whom DIY means helping yourself to a house and for whom property ladders are a means of getting into somebody else's. They are the squatters: idlers handy with a hammer, naysayers to the home-owning norm.

Thatcher, According to a popular misconception, vanquished the squatters, wielding her Criminal Justice Act, in 1994. She didn't; they hid. Squatters have a penchant for invisibility, anyway. Obscured by the Sitex steel panels on condemned tower blocks, forgotten council flats and disused pubs, they call to mind the Borribles: scruffy street dwellers turned feral creatures with pointy ears in the novels of Michael de Larrabeiti.

Being clandestine, squatters are hard to tally. Officially, they remain an enigma: a recent report from the homelessness charity Crisis says, "Virtually nothing is known about squatting." (Obscurity can suit squatters, for whom detection often means eviction; stay twelve years in a squat and they can even claim "adverse possession" of it themselves.) But the indications are that recruits are once again flocking to this itinerant army. The Advisory Service for Squatters, a voluntary group of hardened and wily non-owner-occupiers and the best source of figures, puts the number of squatters in England and Wales as having risen by 60% since 1995, from 9,500 people to around 15,000. Its phones, it says, have not been so busy since the squatting flare of the late 1970s.

"One of the reasons I squat is because I'm a single white male, and I haven't got a dog's chance in hell of ever getting a council house," says Robbie, 57, a housing activist who has been squatting for more than thirty years. Taking a break from vending *The Big Issue* (he was street-selling *International Times*, a sister paper to *Oz*, in the early

27

70s) at the charity's headquarters beneath the flyover tangle outside Vauxhall Tube station, he elaborates: "I've been on council house waiting lists for over ten years and I'm never going to creep up to the top unless I become disabled and I turn to drugs or alcohol, or become mentally ill, or have something which is going to give me that extra little shove."

People like Robbie could be easily housed. There are 750,000 vacant dwellings around the UK, 3.4% of the housing stock. Even in London, with its ferocious market of the past five years, 3.2% of houses are empty. Tony Blair plans to fill some of these homes as part of his government's much trumpeted plan to "tackle" homelessness.

The squatters may be on the march again but time has changed their complexion. Increasingly often, they are European. Of the 10,000 squatters in London–80% to 90% of the British total–a solid sample have hunkered down at Marlowe House, in Lewisham, in the south-east. Around 350 people occupy 93 squats in these two medium-rise, brown tower blocks, which the council is itching to demolish.

The lobby–damp, with an ancient palimpsest of graffiti and a faint smell of urine–does not provide a good first impression. Nor does the lift, a mutilated cube; and climbing the stairs reveals an inch of inundation along one dark corridor. But the sixth floor has an instantly homelier feel. There are posters urging recycling, and Nico's door has a sign advertising organic muesli.

There is a certain division by floor, as Nico, a Frenchman in his late 20s, explains in the flat he shares with two squatter compatriots; "we're all hippies on the 6th". Most of the people who filled the condemned blocks over the past year have been foreign, he says. Only a fraction of the squatters are British; most are Polish. There was even a Polish website exhorting people from the new EU country to come to the blocks and squat while they looked for the abundant low-wage work on offer in the UK.

"When I first came to England, I didn't know about squatting," Nico explains. "When I discovered [it,] it was like a kind of parallel universe: like Babylon, or the resistance. I really saw through squatting that people were living in a different way. It's a means of choosing my own way. If I don't have to pay rent, I don't need to work 40 hours a week.

"I've made a lot of friends [here]. We help each other with tools. Sometimes the council comes and destroys the flat and you need tools to fix it. I've learned a lot of skills here."

> "IF I DON'T HAVE TO PAY RENT, THEN I DON'T HAVE TO WORK FORTY HOURS A WEEK"

Some squatters see themselves as not just like the resistance but as part of one. A new movement, centred around squatted "social centres" and united by a self-proclaimed anarchist tendency seeks to invigorate the squatting activism of the 70s with technologically savvy creative activity.

The rampART, a former Islamic girls' school on fittingly eponymous Rampart Street in the heart of Bangladeshi east London, is, apparently, a "social space" but, like many squats, seemingly one rather hard to get into. Various Europeans, of indeterminate accent guard the entrance nervously. Eventually, however, on the third floor, at the end of a trail of discarded electronics that begins as a garland of computer guts around the double entrance door (digital scavenging seems *de rigueur* in the squats of today), I find one of the squat's founders, Selene, a German in her 20s.

It is, she proclaims, neither she, nor the squat itself, that is important but rather the coming-together of the various groups (Women of Colour, the Solidarity Group for Bolivia, Green Angels) and the activities (hemp-costume making, classes in open-source software) that it allows. "If the rampART is shut down, we will establish another non-commercial space where people can set up events and speak out on issues that the mainstream media doesn't talk about," she says. Every decision about the squat is made "by consensus, horizontally rather than vertically"; "every voice is equal". Indeed, the air at the rampART is thick with talk of meetings.

The air at a rare, old theatre-in-the-round in north London is thick with middle-class accents, and I only need to note as well the gaily painted signs pointing to all sorts of "spaces" to be reminded that I am in a squat. House on the Rock, a Nigerian Pentecostal church, would very much like to occupy this building, which it recently bought for more than £1m, in order to rededicate it–it was originally a church–to the greater glory of God. The illicit resident who chimes "hello!" as she swings past on a trapeze suspended from the great, vaulted ceiling of the auditorium, is just one of ten members of the Earth Circus, a roving, squatting troupe, in the church's way.

The evangelists have proposed a compromise whereby the circus would be able to perform in the auditorium for a few hours a week, but its pre-emptive ban on obscenity, violence or gay references sticks in the libertarian craw of one of the occupiers, Susanna Lafond, 60, a "druid" and

THE SQUATTERS HANDBOOK

The Squatter's Handbook is like a *Little Red Book* for the squatting movement. Published by the Advisory Service for Squatters and in its 12th edition, it seeks to tell you everything you need to know to be a successful squatter–all in a jeans-pocket-sized manual costing £2.

Where to Squat?

Plan ahead: don't "lucky dip" squat. Local authority owned "empties" used to be the best bet but these have increasingly been sold off; councils have also become more hardline towards squatters, with a tendency to "gut" vulnerable properties. Aim instead, for houses awaiting renovation or demolition. "Lots of commercial property is being squatted at the moment," too, the handbook says, particularly pubs, but beware: the owners are unpredictable and sometimes "send in the heavies". Not sure if a place is occupied? "Try sticking a hair held by two small blobs of superglue across the bottom of the door opening." Don't squat holiday homes.

Moving In

Don't try to batter down the front door; go round the back. Bring tools, and if the police should stop you in the street, tell an environmental activist of long-standing. She calls the occupation of the building "politics at a very grass-roots level. We are activating a space which has sat here empty for four years, which is a sin! The council can't do it, because it has no money. We're saying, this is how we do it, guys, with no money."

Maureen and her husband, Peter are mater–and paterfamilias to a shifting group of around seven squatters who have hauled their "kit" about on Peter's milkfloat for a decade–to half a dozen squats in the past year alone. Their current digs are an ex-pub, the Eagle and Child, on the edge of Epping Forest, in east London.

Their living room is the expansive, former saloon bar, illuminated by the milky, winter light from the one window lacking a bolted-on metal blind. Salvaged computers skirt the walls; a bright but ill-fitting square of carpet and the sofas clustered around it are also reclaimed from the streets. Above the setting hangs a big mirror, amid a spiral of fairy lights. Peter started squatting in his home village, in Norfolk, 15 or 20 years ago now and has "just kept doing it". Maureen has been squatting for 10 years, but "is getting a bit old for all this moving".

"People think squatting's an easy lifestyle," Peter says. "Well, it ain't. Because you don't move into a place where someone's just gone on holiday for a couple of weeks. They're places that people have abandoned or that are up for demolition in six months, a year. There's nothing there. There's no plumbing, no wiring, huge holes in the roof. Floors have been chopped out. You've got to be able to put it right, because you can't afford to employ a tradesman. It's exciting. Driving somewhere, getting in, setting up. Normal life is boring, isn't it?"

In shirking the idol of home-ownership, the squatters set a rare and valuable example. As Robbie, the veteran squatter, says: "I think society has a lot to learn from squatters. As people are rejected from the system, they create an alternative, and the alternative often works far better than the *status quo*."

them your crowbar is for "clearing the drains". Don't frighten the neighbours; get in during the day. Wear workmen's overalls. Change the lock: diagrams in the handbook show you how.

DIY

Check the utility supplies: water is the hardest to live without. Be careful of dried pigeon shit: it's poisonous to breathe in. Become an amateur electrician, because electricity can kill. If someone should suffer a shock, have a broomstick on hand to remove them from the current.

GETTING SETTLED

Make the place look lived in. Have someone home 24 hours a day, otherwise it will be easier to evict you. Should your door always be open to other, needy squatters? Not necessarily, but "think carefully before you exclude anyone. Everybody has a right to a home–that is the basic principle of the squatting movement."

Currency & The Guilds

In Medieval times there was a great revolution in everyday life. The common man rebelled against the rule of the nobles and built their own cities and cathedrals. Operating under a Catholic Christian set of moral guidelines, they set up Guilds of craftspeople to end exploitation. The following essay, published in 1923, was written by one of a group of Catholic intellectuals in the early 20th century who searched for alternatives to the modern working system of wage slavery and debt.

It is a commonly held opinion that gains some support from the theory of Roman law that civilisation owes its existence to the introduction of slavery. Such a view, however, is untenable. It recieves no support from the actual facts, for we know that slavery existed long before civilisation came into existence. Not slavery, but the introduction of currency was the decisive factor in the situation; and it is the failure to understand this fact that is one of the root causes of confusion in social theory. It cannot fail to strike the impartial observer as an extraordinary thing that currency, to the introduction of which civilisation owes its very existence, should have no recognised place in social theory. Yet such is the case. Its problems, which are central in civilisation, are treated as the mere technical ones of bankers and financiers, and are only approached from their point of view. But the bankers'

MARY EVANS PICTURE LIBRARY

THIS 1923 ESSAY EXPLAINS HOW THE MEDIEVAL GUILD SYSTEM DEALT WITH THE PROBLEM OF MONEY. BY ARTHUR J PENTY

approach is most demonstrably a fundamentally false one; for it ignores the moral issue involved in such hopeless confusion. For currency, like every other social and economic problem, to be intelligible must be approached historically, in the light of a definite moral standard, and not as being a purely technical question of men who are familiar with the intricacies of finance.

Currency was first introduced in the seventh century before Christ, when the Lydian kings introduced stamped bars of fixed weight to replace the metal bars of unfixed weight which hitherto had served as a medium of exchange. It was a simple device the consequences of which were entirely unforeseen; but the developments that followed upon it were simply stupendous. It created an economic revolution comparable only to that which followed the invention of the steam engine in more recent times. Civilisation–that is, the development of the material accessories of life–dates from that simple invention; for by facilitating exchange it made possible differentiation of occupation, specialisation in the crafts and arts, city life and foreign trade. But along with the undoubted advantages which a fixed currency brought with it, there came an evil unknown to primitive society–the economic problem. For the introduction of currency not only undermined the common life of the Mediterranean communities, but it brought into existence the problem of capitalism. And with capitalism there came the division of society into two distinct and hostile classes–the prosperous land-owners, merchants and money-lending class on the one hand, and the peasantry and debt slaves on the other, while incidentally it gave rise to the private ownership of land, which now for the first time could be bought and sold as a commodity.

The reason for these developments is not far to seek. So long as the exchange was carried on by barter a natural limit was placed to the development of trade, because under such circumstances people would only exchange wares for their own personal use. Exchange would only be possible when each party to the bargain possessed some article of which the other was in need. But with the introduction of currency, circumstances changed, and for the first time in history there came into existence a class of men who bought and sold entirely for the purposes of gain. These merchants or middlemen became specialists in finance. They knew better than the peasantry the market value of things, and so they found little difficulty in taking advantage of them. Little by little they became rich and the peasantry their debtors. It is the same story wherever men are at liberty to speculate in values and exchange is unregulated–the distributor enslaves the producer. It happened in Greece, it happened in Rome, and it has happened everywhere in the modern world, for speculation in exchange brings in its train the same evils.

Though the Greeks and the Romans thought a great deal about the economic problems that had followed the introduction of currency, to the end the problem eluded them. The ideal of Plato of rebuilding a society anew on the principles of justice gave way to the more immediately practical aim of the Roman jurists of maintaining order. For, as I have previously pointed out, the maintenance of order rather than justice was the aim of Roman law, and as such it was an instrument for holding together a society that had been rendered unstable by the growth of capitalism. Thus we see there is a definite connection between the development of Roman civil law and the inability of antiquity to find a solution for the problems of currency. Freedom of exchange having led to capitalism, and capitalism to social disorders, Roman law stepped into the breach, and by legislating injustices sought to preserve order. And because of this, because of the generally received opinion in Rome that injustice was necessarily involved in the administration of the commonwealth, the jurists of the Antonine period came to postulate the Law of Nature in order to provide a philosophic basis for their legal measures of practical necessity. And as reform activities have ever since the Middle Ages been influenced by the Law of Nature, we see that the vicious circle in which they move owes its existence to the general failure to give the problem of currency its position of central importance.

Unregulated currency gradually disintegrated the civilizations of Greece and Rome, and mankind had to wait until the Middle Ages before a solution was forthcoming, when it was provided by the Guilds in the light of the teaching of Christianity, though owing to the fact that the Guilds came into existence as spontaneous and instinctive creations of the people, their significance was entirely overlooked by Medieval thinkers, who, if orthodox, confined their social and politicial speculations to the range of issues covered by the Civil and Canon Laws, and, if revolutionary, to the issues raised by the Law of Nature, in neither of which systems Guilds found a place. This was one of the tragedies of the Middle Ages. For in organising the Guilds the townsmen of the Middle Ages unconsciously stumbled upon the solution of the problem of currency, but owing to the fact that the minds of thinkers and publicists of the time were engrossed with other things the social potentialities of this great discovery were lost to the world.

THE TOWNSMEN STUMBLED ON THE SOLUTION OF THE PROBLEM OF CURRENCY

THE IDEA WAS TO STABILISE CURRENCY BY THE INSTITUTION OF A JUST AND FIXED PRICE

What then was the solution provided by the Guilds? It was to stablilise currency by the institution of a Just and Fixed price. The Just price had a central place in Medieval economic theory, though, strictly speaking, the Just price is a moral rather than an economic idea. The Medievalists understood what we are only beginning to understand–that there is no such thing as a purely economic solution of the problems of society, since economics are not to be understood as a separate and detached science considered apart from morals. On the contrary, economic issues are primarily moral issues with economic equivalents. And for this reason Medievalists insisted upon things being bought and sold at a Just Price. They taught that to buy a thing for less or to sell a thing for more than its real value was in itself unallowable and unjust, and therefore sinful, though exceptional circumstances might at times make it permissible. The institution of buying and selling was established for the common advantage of mankind, but the ends of justice and equality were defeated if one party to any transaction received a price that was more and the other less than the article was worth.

This doctrine–that wares should be sold at a Just Price–together with another–that the taking of interest was sinful–was insisted upon by the Church, and obedience was enforced from the pulpit, in the confessional, and in the ecclesiastical courts. So effectively were these doctrines impressed upon the consciences of men that their principles found their way into all the secular legislation of the period, whether of Parliament, Guild or Municipality. The differing fortunes that followed these legislative attempts to secure obedience to the principles of the Just Price is instructive, for it demonstrates the undoubted superiority of the Guild as an instrument for the performance of economic functions.

Parliament could do nothing but enact laws against profiteering, and, as such, its actions were negative and finally ineffective. But the Guilds were positive. They sought to give effect to the principle of the Just Price by making it at the same time a Fixed price, and around this central idea there was gradually built up the wonderful system of the corporate life of the cities. Thus, in order to perform their economic functions, the Guilds had to be privileged bodies, having a complete monopoly of their trades over the area of a particular town or city; for only through the exercise of authority over its individual members could a Guild enforce a discipline. Profiteering and other trade abuses were ruthlessly suppressed; for the first offence a member was fined; the most severe penalty was expulsion from the Guild, when a man lost the privilege of following his trade or craft in his native city.

But a Just and Fixed price cannot be maintained by moral action alone. If prices are to be fixed thoughout industry, it can only be on the assumption that a standard of quality can be upheld. As a standard of quality cannot be defined in terms of law, it is necessary, for the maintenance of a standard, to place authority in the hands of craftmasters, a consensus of whose opinion constitutes the final court of appeal. In order to ensure a supply of masters it is necessary to train apprentices, to regulate the size of the workshop, the hours of labour, the volume of production, and so forth; for only when attention is given to such matters is it possible "to ensure the permanency of practice and continuity of tradition, whereby alone the reputation of the Guild for honourable dealing and sound workmanship can be carried on from generation to generation," and conditions created favourable to the production of masters. Thus we see all the regulations–as indeed the whole hierarchy of the Guilds–arising out of the primary object of maintaining the Just Price.

But it will be said: If the Medieval Guilds were such excellent institutions, why did they disappear? The immediate cause is to be found in the fact that they were not co-extensive in society. The Guilds existed in the towns, but they never came into existence in the rural areas. That was the weak place in the Medieval economic armour; for it is obvious that if a Fixed Price was finally maintained anywhere, it would have to be maintained everywhere, both in town and country. That Guilds were never organised in rural areas is to be explained immediately by the fact that in the eleventh and twelfth centuries, when the Guilds were organised in the towns, the agricultural population was organised under Feudalism, and money was only beginning to be used, so the problem was not pressing. But the ultimate reason is to be found in the fact that the impossiblity of maintaining, in the long run, a Just Price that was not a Fixed Price was not at the time appreciated by the Church, which appears to have been blind to the need of Guild organization for its maintenance. Churchmen then thought, as so many do today, that the world can be redeemed by moral action alone, never realising that a high standard of commercial morality can only be maintained if organisations exist to suppress a lower one. Hence, it came about that, when in the thirteenth century the validity of the Just Price came to be challenged by lawyers, who maintained the right of every man to make the best bargain he could for himself, the moral sanction on which the maintenance of the Just Price ultimately rested was undermined. Belief in it lost hold on the country population, and then the Guild regulations

came to be regarded as unnecessary restrictions of the freedom of the individual. Thus a way was opened in rural areas for the growth of capitalism and speculation, and this made it increasingly difficult for the Guilds to maintain fixed prices in the towns until at last, in the sixteenth century, the whole system broke down amid the economic chaos that followed the suppression of the monasteries and the wholesale importation of gold from South America, which doubled prices all over Europe. It was because the Guilds were unable to perform any longer the functions that brought them into existence that they finally fell, and not because of the Chantries Act of 1547. This Act did not

IN THE 16TH CENTURY THE WHOLE SYSTEM BROKE DOWN FOLLOWING THE SUPPRESSION OF THE MONASTERIES

attack the Guilds as economic organizations, as is commonly supposed, nor did it seek to confiscate the whole of their property, but only such part of their revenues as had already been devoted to specified religious purpose.

The explanation I have given of the decline of the Guilds is, so far as the details are concerned, the history of the decline of the English Guilds only. On the Continent, the decline pursued a

different course, and as the factors in the situation were there much more complex, it is not so easy to generalize. Nevertheless, I think it is true to say that the ultimate cause of their decline is to be traced to the revival of Roman law. The Guilds went down not because they were unfitted by their nature to grapple with the problems of a wider social intercourse, as historians have too hastily assumed, but because the moral sanctions on which they rested had been completely undermined by the revival of a system of law that gave legal sanction to usury and permitted speculation in prices. Unfortunately, the truth of the matter, which is extremely simple, has been concealed from the public by a mysterious habit of economic historians of always talking about the growth of national industry, when what they really mean is the growth of capitalist industry. If they talked about the growth of capitalist industry, everyone would understand that the failure of the Guilds was a consequence of the moral failure of Medieval society, for the issues would be clear. But instead of talking about capitalist industry, they talk about national industry, and people are led to suppose that the Guilds declined because their type of organization became obsolete, which is not the case, as we shall later see.

From *The Gauntlet: A Challenege to the Myth of Progress* by Arthur J. Penty (IHS Press)

STORIES

Waterloo

By Stewart Home
Illustrations by Hannah Dyson

I arrived in London from the west country, but that is not important. What mattered was that my education was complete. I had both a foundation and a BA in fine art. I was fully qualified and believed that I'd conceived the perfect crime. Perfect not because it was victimless, but rather due to the fact that those I intended to dupe stood to benefit both financially and culturally from their flagrant credulity. Having read Machiavelli, or rather a short introduction to his thought, I believed that self-interest was the ruling motive in human affairs.

I arrived at Waterloo station carrying a backpack on my shoulders and a large suitcase in each hand. I walked off the platform and five minutes later I was established in my furnished–albeit sparsely–flat. The Cut, according to a rumour long spread by both estate agents and those who owned property in the immediate vicinity, was up and coming. Indeed, it had been up and coming for the past thirty years. It took no time at all to walk to Waterloo Bridge, and across the river lay the West End, which was where those who could afford it chose to live. That said, I was central enough for journalists to flock to my digs.

My plan was simple, but there was no point in carrying it off anywhere other than London. A provincial town would not do, and since I spoke neither Dutch nor German, I decided against Amsterdam or Berlin. Paris was too chic and New York too far away. No, I preferred dirty, money-

BEFORE LONG, CRITICS WERE FALLING OVER EACH OTHER TO WRITE ABOUT MY ART

grubbing, boorish London, with its cod neo-conceptual art and the inescapable sense the city gave of having a permanent hangover. The art buzz had moved elsewhere, which was fine by me, since I intended to take the credit for making London swing again. I wanted to produce an art that would draw crowds the likes of which hadn't been seen since the Tyburn gallows was dismantled.

I set to work at once getting to know some of those who retailed goods from shops and market stalls in Lower Marsh Street. I didn't need to rush things since between housing benefit and social security I wasn't going to starve in my garret, although a bit of spare cash to pay for luxuries like heating wouldn't have gone amiss. When talking to my new friends I let everyone know I was an artist. Generally such revelations were treated with derision. Nonetheless when I showed local traders my drawings of bank notes, they found it easy enough to relate to my work.

"Not bad, dear," a lady who ran a clothes stall told me after glancing at a pen and ink sketch of a twenty pound note, "but I prefer the original because that's the only thing which will pay for my lottery tickets."

"I'd swap it for a pair of jeans," I suggested hopefully.

"I'll give you some Wranglers, and you can pay me when you get your giro." Bertha was incapable of understanding that art was an investment.

It took quite some time but eventually the local traders caught on to my scam. I would invite art critics to Lower Marsh Street and amaze them with the accomplished fact of my success at exchanging drawings of currency for consumer goods. All told nearly a dozen shopkeepers and market stall traders assisted me in pulling the wool over the eyes of art world curmudgeons. We worked out a system of credit whereby I'd pay my debts by instalment and when I'd covered the cost of the goods I'd taken plus fifty percent, I'd get my drawings back.

John Garland was the first critic to visit me at what I called my studio, in actuality a café on Lower Marsh Street. Using a commercial eatery not only saved me the expense of renting a work space, it was simultaneously a sassy publicity gimmick. As for John Garland, he was a highly ambitious art critic who talked endlessly (and it must be added incoherently) about philistinism, the everyday and the self-reflexivity of art. Garland had assimilated, without understanding, the theories of Theodor Adorno and the Frankfurt School. Regardless of Garland's defective grasp of aesthetic theory, the regular appearance of his prose in the art press made him the ideal man to promote my work. Of course, I wasn't surprised that Garland made me barter for his praise.

"I'll give you a big spread in one of the monthlies," Garland promised, "if you can introduce me to a chick who likes football and is gagging for it."

"Gagging for it?"

"You know, supports Leyton Orient and would like to sit in bed with me, without any clothes on, watching Match Of The Day while we share a packet of

prawn cocktail crisps."

"Oh, you mean someone like Tracey Emin, only not as famous."

"Precisely!"

"I'm afraid," and I was loath to admit it, "I don't know anyone who supports Orient."

"What about Tracey Emin?"

"I don't know her."

"Well, are you sure she supports Leyton?"

"I dunno, she's from Kent, I'd imagine she supports Gillingham."

"Gillingham's play is crudely identitary and this contrasts sharply with Orient's brilliant heterogeneity, which expresses the idea of harmony negatively by embodying contradictions pure and uncompromised in its innermost structure. In the end, Gillingham produce what all positivists produce, an eradication of the subject as agent."

"Right!" I concurred.

Garland was happy enough with the mere affirmation of his views, which cost me little even in terms of commitment to his *weltanschauung*, since his opinions were stuff and nonsense. I went on to assure Garland I knew a woman who was desperate to fuck a *bona fide* art critic, and that if he'd wait in my flat, I'd send her up. I don't think Garland ever worked out that the girl he shagged was a prostitute who I paid to do the business with him. The upshot of all this was that I got a three page feature in a small circulation monthly magazine.

The coverage of my work built steadily from this humble beginning and before long, critics were falling over each other to write about my art. However it was not until after I was awoken by a loud hammering on the door about ten o'clock one morning that I briefly deluded myself into thinking I'd finally arrived. I was in bed with a girl called Gail Sanders

who I'd met down the pub the previous night. Initially my heart sunk when three men whose knuckles reached down to the floor flashed search warrants in my face. It was only after they'd pushed their way into the flat that I realised they belonged to the Forgery Squad. Since my work had been widely reproduced in the art press I didn't see why the law needed to turn over my drum but once they'd located a few of my currency drawings they appeared satisfied.

The rozzers were rather amused by my activities and after we'd shared a pot of tea they left saying I'd have my day in court. I felt so happy I shook all three cops by the hand, since not even real money could buy the type of publicity that it then appeared was about to come my way. None the less when the law left I felt a palpable sense of relief that they hadn't found the various human body parts I had stashed in my freezer. I'd stolen limbs, heads and torsos from various mortuaries with the intention of reinventing myself as a sculptor of macabries at some point in the not too distant future. It was Gail Sanders who put the shakes back into me.

"They can't possibly be doing you for forgery. I saw the drawings they took and they're about as convincing as pieces of currency as a child's play money. That must have been a fishing expedition, they're after something else. If your drawings are forgeries then I'm the Queen Of Sheba!"

If I'd only consulted a lawyer then I'd have discovered that the British Forgery Act was so comprehensive that to reproduce a mere segment of any currency from anywhere in the world was a serious crime. Since my money pictures had appeared in the art press what I'd been up to amounted to a conspiracy and therefore carried a minimum jail term of two years. Unfortunately, instead of seeking legal advice I panicked. I showed Gail the human remains in my freezer and asked her to help me dispose of them in some bins at the back of Waterloo railway station. Sanders ran screaming from the flat. I followed her down the stairs but soon lost her in the bustling street outside.

Rather than immediately going underground with some trusted art contacts in Tumbridge Wells who over the years had safe housed a a number of cultural workers who'd found themselves in trouble with the law, I went back to my flat to dispose of the body parts. Gail must have gone straight to the cops because I was busted by dozens of heavily armed detectives as I wrapped the left leg of a teenage female in a plastic bin liner. Six months later I made my appearance at the number one court of the Old Bailey. The trail was over so quickly it barely made the papers and since I was unable to prove I'd stolen the body parts, I was committed to Broadmoor as a dangerously deranged serial killer. Much to my annoyance I got off the forgery charge on a technicality. After my conviction I was classified as mentally unfit to stand trial on any other charges. A forgery case would have cemented my reputation within the cultural industry. Unfortunately nobody in a position of power within the art world wants anything to do with someone like me who's been wrongly branded a psychotic. Recently I've been spending my days on a locked ward where to pass the time I paint pictures in the style of the Old Masters. As forgeries these are considerably more convincing than the twenty pound notes I used to draw when I lived in Waterloo.

THE LONG-TAILED TIT.

Aegithalos caudatus.

Under-side of tail.

P. Beer.

The Chronicles of Peregrine Beer

Being the next instalment in the adventures of Britain's most drunken birdwatcher. Story and illustration by Jock Scot

Having decided to accept a lift back to London with The Libertonies instead of returning in the RSPB coach, Perry was rueing that spur-of-the-moment decision by the time they roared through Carshalton. The appalling behaviour and argumentative nature of his travelling companions in the Transit van had made the journey a nightmare. They were drunk to a man but The Libertonies, apart from Pedro, were not holding their drink at all well and were behaving like a trio of 15-year-olds, drunk for the very first time. Their charming continental manners had deserted them and they chose to communicate in a series of silly voices, rude noises and hysterical laughter, pulling faces all the while. "Just drop me off at the next tube station!" pleaded Perry as they screeched round another roundabout on two wheels.

Positioned as he was in the back of the van, facing in the opposite direction to the one they were travelling in, he was spared the visual evidence of Mal's drunken driving. Pedro lay beside him on the flightcase and, despite the noise and the language barrier, by miming the words they couldn't speak, they bonded.

The Transit left the North Circular at the Golder's Green exit and headed down to Kilburn and tonight's gig at "The Mean Scotsman." Mal pulled up outside and they began unloading the gear. Perry wandered into the bar and ordered a pint of Guinness, closely followed by Pedro.

"I'm just gonna nip round to my brother's flat for a clean shirt and a cup of tea. Would you care to accompany me? I should get out these pyjamas." They drained their pints and left the bar, on the way up Kilburn High Road they visited an off-licence for more fags and a few cans.

Perry rang the doorbell and they waited, a curtain twitched and was drawn back to reveal the gurning, highly mobile face of Perry's brother, Shed.

THE SMALL PARTY OF SEVEN BIRDS CLIMBED NIMBLY, SEARCHING FOR INSECTS, APHIDS AND SPIDERS

"Open up you old tart and get the kettle on!" roared Perry. Soon enough, after an unlocking routine involving much throwing back of bolts, clinking of chains cursing and banging, the front door opened and the brothers embraced.

"Come in! Come in, Perry, dear boy! And who is this little poppet with you?" said the tenant brother.

"Meet my new best friend Pedro. Pedro, my brother Shed, a keen gardener and a font of knowledge regarding superstition. Shed, Pedro is a travelling musician of Italian extraction currently handling lead vocal duties for The Libertonies, a popular tribute band".

"Delighted to make your acquaintance. I'm a musician myself, I play the bagpipes. Neighbours always complaining. Philistines. Come in, come in. Perry, whatever are you wearing? Just as well Mum isn't here, she'd give you a thick ear".

"One of the reasons for our spontaneous visit, Shed. I badly need a change of clothes. I left home in a bit of a hurry."

"So I see, sit yourselves down and I'll put the kettle on."

Pedro looked around the lounge for a seat, finally spotting a deckchair amidst the bohemian clutter. He shifted the set of bagpipes nestling there, sat down and surveyed his surroundings. The room was a curious amalgam of library, junk shop and *ad hoc* living quarters. The kindest way to describe it would be to say that it seemed to lack a woman's touch. Above the fireplace a large-framed Jamie Reid print of a kneeling sweater-girl, bearing the legend "Sex Pistols Fuck Forever" tried to dominate the room. Close to one hundred framed photos and prints hung on the walls from waist height to ceiling: a catholic mixture of Shed's literary and sporting heroes and historical figures, haphazardly hung in a rogues gallery hall of fame.

Shed returned with a tea tray, trouserings and tee shirt. He set the tray down. The trouserings were camouflaged combat in fashion; the tee shirt bright red with CUBA in white letters across the front. He chucked the clothes to Perry saying,

"Will those suit?"

"My outlandish outfit has served me well this day, but I fear that a visit to the Mean Scotsman to witness a concert performance by The Libertonies will require something of a different cut. I shall go as Che Guevara! Do you possess a beret, Shed? My dearest brother and comrade, a beret is what is required at this juncture, to set off the Cuba tee-shirt and the camouflaged combat fatigue trouserings."

"Oh! Was there a fifty pound note in the pocket of the jacket–the jacket you borrowed last time?" asked Shed, answering a question with another question.

Perry sipped his tea and shot his brother a quizzical look.

"I'll sort you out later, bit short of ready cash at the moment. Shed, you are neglecting your continental visitor, young Pedro looks thirsty in the extreme.

"Oh! Terribly sorry, mon brave! Would you like something stronger, Pedro, a wee dram perhaps? I have a bottle of Cameron Brig which I've been keeping for a special occasion. Shall we go into the garden, quite a pleasant evening, I could give you a tune on the pipes".

"Excellent, Shed! I could do with a small refreshment, we brought a few cans with us," said the ever-thirsty Perry.

They traipsed out to the back garden and Shed conducted his visitors round and gave a running commentary. They walked beneath palm trees and eucalyptus, some oriental poppies, bright red, caught the eye, contrasting sharply with the blue poppy, mecanopsis sheldonii, and, in a large group at the back of the garden, papaver somniverum, the opium poppy.

After the guided tour they reclined in deck chairs on the patio and savoured the Cameron Brig. It is a unique patent-still grain whisky, the only one of that type now on the market. Clear and sharp in taste, almost antiseptic in character, there's nothing else like it.

Shed poured generous measures and initiated gay banter.

"So tell me Pedro, how do you find the United Kingdom, enjoying your visit?"

"Your country has been much enjoyment, I especially like the Tennants Super lager. But my friends in the van have not been so flavour. They are like bambinos and not take the music any good. They are jazz musicians at home and no like English punk rock. I am liking very much to be here, away from they."

"Never mind, son, you're among friends here," said Shed reassuringly.

"Don't move lads. We have visitors."

Perry pointed to a group of small birds which had alighted in the nearest eucalyptus. They were small, black and white with long thin tails.

"Long-tailed tits" whispered Perry with authority. "Look at the tail, unmistakeable." The small birds did indeed have long tails and as a pair drew apart from the main group, chasing a feather as it floated to the ground, Perry drew their attention to the pink feathers among the black and white plumage. Close up, the small tits were quite beautiful. Perry wanted to cradle them gently in his hands, stroke them, kiss them.

"What a beautiful pair of little tits!" he exclaimed and went into one.

"Not often seen in gardens. Also called the Bottle-tit, from the shape of its domed nest, lays between seven and twelve eggs, that's a lot, so they've got to be little! When the chicks hatch it can get chummy in the nest. The parent birds have to fold their long tails over the back of their heads when they go inside. They don't sing, but go "Zup" and a thin chirp "Si - Si - Si". The tail is gradated, black and white, three inches long, the bird itself measuring only five and a half inches in total."

The small party of seven birds climbed nimbly, searching for insects, aphids and spiders, often hanging upside down. Among their number were two with white heads, the others all had a black, curved, supraorbital stripe, like a Dickensian clerk's quill ink pen tucked behind his ear. They were utterly beautiful.

"Give us a tune on your pipes, dear Shed, brother o' mine. Bring a tear to my eye, what?"

To Be Continued...

Christian Rescues Martin From The Slough of Despond

BY NICHOLAS LEZARD
ILLUSTRATIONS BY EVA-KAJSA HEDSTROM

Martin cracked on the sixth day and called his friend Christian.

"I'm bored," he said. "I'm so bored it's not funny. You've got to come down."

"I thought you were down there to finish your book." Christian spoke the last three words as if they were in inverted commas.

"Oh, don't be a cunt, just get down here. I don't have a car, there's no telly, mobiles don't work in the valley, I'm absolutely fucking sick of log fires and cooking with an Aga. You love all that shit. And bring some grass with you while you're at it. And anything else that's knocking around. I tell you, I'm going crazy down here."

"Marty, it was very silly of you to think you had the brains to finish a book."

"Will you stop that? Just get down here. I need amusement fast." Later that day, with Christian's disgusting Vauxhall parked in the driveway of the ancient cottage, the two friends smoked a large spliff in front of the fire. All around them were books, scattered papers, and several filthy plates and wine-glasses.

"If you were that bored, you could have picked the place up a bit," said Christian.

"Clean it up yourself if it bothers you. Anyway, it's my fucking house."

"No it's not, it's your sister's. And she'd do her nut if she saw it looking like this."

"Absolutely."

"Point taken. Anyway, is there no other human company at all round here?"

"Only the idiots down at the local pub," groaned Martin, "and once you saw them, you wouldn't use the word 'human' lightly again. They're some kind of half-sheep hybrid, but not in any interesting way."

"Tell me more."

"That's literally all there is to say."

"Come, come, you're meant to be the writer. You should be interested in all sentient creatures."

"I tell you, they're not sentient. Look, I've been down there every night but I couldn't face going there again, that's the main reason I called you. It's one of those family places, everything's been done up

MARTIN FOUND HIMSELF SWIFTLY RETREATING INTO PARANOIA

nicely, and now that Christmas is only six weeks away they've put up tinsel and little fucking Santas everywhere, and the families have started bringing in their children and everything to have meals. And the children. They're even fatter than their fucking parents."

"Crowded, then, is it?"

"It gets half-full by about nine. After that I can't take any more conversation about the weather or the wogs in Europe, they really use that word and about Europeans too, it's unbelievable, and you can't even read a book because they play this ghastly music over the PA. I once asked them to turn it down but the barman said the other customers liked it, and he turned it up."

"Other customers?"

"They're the dregs. The best ones are the farm hands, because they don't actually have enough brains to start a sentence, let alone finish one. It's the farmers and the salesmen who you've got to watch out for. They speak their minds and they're frightening. They only barely tolerate me because my sister hasn't sold the family home yet. If I told them I lived in London they'd forget their gentle ways and clobber me to death with a pitchfork or something on the spot. As for the women, they're all witches, there's no other explanation for them. Although if I was in league with the Dark Arts the first thing I'd do is make myself look a little bit more attractive than they do. I'd respect them if they had the imagination or initiative to burn me to death in a Whicker Man but that's just not going to happen. They're more brutal than that. Some comedian made a crop circle in a field up the road last summer and even though it was obviously made by a pissed man with a plank and a rope I noticed that they were still going on about it last night. Having heard what they think about the French I shudder to think what they'd do to ET if he showed up here. But I suppose my only realistic fear obliges me to finish my pint before I go for a piss, because it means I don't have to worry about someone spitting in my glass before I get back."

"Tsk, tsk."

"It got so bad that last night on the way back I tried to have a conversation with a sheep, because I noticed that when a sheep says 'baa' it sounds very like a human being doing a good impersonation of a sheep. So one of them went baa and none of his mates answered him, so I went baa just to get the ball rolling and you know what? The conversation ended right there. That's when I realized I was going a bit nuts."

"You should, perhaps, treat the locals with a little more indulgence."

"No, the short chat with the sheep was really a bit of a highlight. I tell you, the people in the pub are frightful."

"Sounds like they need a little bit of shaking up," said Christian.

"You're not thinking of going down there, are you?"

"What, you want to stay here and play Scrabble?"

"Oh, there's no Scrabble in this house. My sister couldn't make a word out of the letters c, a, and t, and she's a towering intellect compared to her husband."

Martin could never bring himself to mention him by name.

"Have you considered going to another

pub? An obvious question, but allow me to put it to you."

"This is the only one in walking distance."

"Get a cab."

"You think I'm getting in a car for more than five minutes with one of these maniacs? I've seen *Deliverance*."

"Well," said Christian, with a theatrical little sigh, "let's see what there is in this house, then."

Lakedean Cottage had been in Martin's family for three generations, but Martin's sister took great pride in regular clearouts, so the inspection didn't take long. Interior decoration was largely limited to photographs of the sister getting married, or wearing big hats at racecourses, and a mounted set of pre-decimal currency ordered from an advertisement in the *Radio Times*. The only books which weren't Martin's (which were themselves severely academic) were an ancient bound set of *Punch*, an obviously untouched complete Dickens, and *Could Try Harder*, a collection of minor celebrities' school reports, which was in the downstairs loo.

"Not big readers, my ancestors," said Martin.

"Fucking hell," agreed Christian. "Let's have a look in the wardrobes."

They found absolutely nothing of interest in them, until they came to the end room, a damp, freezing chamber of such evil aspect that it had obviously been unused almost since the place's first occupation. But in the wardrobe was a musty-smelling frock-coat, waistcoat, and sponge-bag trousers.

"Aha," said Christian. A black-hearted idea was taking shape.

"What time is it?"

"About seven-thirty."

"Splendid. Time for a little nerve tonic, a line of two to give one heart and suppress the giggles, and a little smoke for balance, then we'll be off. While you're preparing the necessary, I'm going to try these on for size."

The tailcoat and its accompaniments fitted him only just within the bounds of complete eccentricity. He turned the collar of his shirt up and tousled his hair. From a strip of black silk found in the sister's dressing-table he fashioned a bootlace tie with flamboyant bows.

"There. How do I look?"

"You look like a fucking lunatic," said Martin.

"Excellent."

They settled down to their medication. Christian expanded and relaxed even further; Martin, even though he had craved precisely the kind of company which his old friend so reliably provided, found himself swiftly retreating into paranoia. This often happened when he was with Christian, he reflected, and it didn't even always need drugs.

"What's the plan, then?" he asked miserably.

"Your part in it is simple. We park the car around a convenient corner. You go in, buy yourself a drink, and hang about the bar looking a bit spooked. You look as though you should be able to manage that very well."

Martin agreed.

"Five minutes later I'll come in. Try not to be too visibly alarmed at my aspect."

"Too late, I'm already alarmed."

"Well, anyway, the important thing is that you don't know me."

"God, if only."

"Very funny. Now, at one point I will look you right in the eye and ask you a question. I won't tell you now, it'll spoil the surprise. But what you have to do is reply: 'now you come to mention it, yes.' Got that? Repeat those words."

Martin obliged.

"I suppose that'll have to do. The monotone may even work in our favour. One more thing that's just occurred to me–are there any stone circles or barrows near here?"

"This is Wiltshire. You can't have a slash against a hedge without stubbing your toe on a dolmen."

"Perfect. Now, one last enormous line, and we'll be off. Oh, what's your sister's home number?"

"Look, what are you going to do? Why the hell do you want that?"

"I'm afraid the element of surprise is crucial. Number, please."

"Are we going to get into trouble?"

"That depends on the native good sense of the good yeoman stock of this village. If they have any, we're fucked. But from what you tell me, we should be OK."

"Is anyone going to get hurt?"

"Well, we might, but only if we go back there tomorrow. I'm the only one at any real risk. Look, all I'm going to do is liven everyone up and expose them to the elements for a while. Let's hope they're wrapped up warm. Oh, one last thing–is there an ordnance survey map of the area here?"

"What for?" Martin was beginning to become seriously rattled by the wild, committed look in his friend's eye.

"Just show me." Christian scrutinized it for a few seconds. "The great thing about ley lines," he said, "is that you can make them up so easily. That's us, yes? Excellent. Let's go. Put the map in your pocket. Oh, silly me, nearly forgot." He walked over to the display of pre-decimal coins, smashed the glass, and emptied the extinct currency into his pocket.

"What the fuck are you doing, Christian?" shrieked Martin.

"Can't go out without any cash," said Christian. They parked round the corner. Christian had wanted to drive the short distance without lights–"silent running", he pleaded, but Martin drew the line at driving even a few hundred yards on a greasy, blustery evening without any illumination.

"Quite a few in tonight, it seems," said Christian, peering at the windows as they passed. "Okay, out you get. Remember your instructions."

Martin had no problem complying with the injunction to look a bit spooked. In fact, he surpassed it: he looked positively haunted. He had craved respite from tedium, and so had called Christian; but he had forgotten how his friend had a far higher threshold of embarrassment than anyone else he knew. It was like he wasn't even English. Christian, he realized, was capable of anything, and trying to work out what he was capable of doing in the next few minutes made Martin's hand tremble so much that he spilled a quarter of his beer on the counter before it was even halfway to his lips. The barmaid scowled at him as she wiped up the mess. A few of the regulars snickered at Martin, and one said something which Martin couldn't decipher, but which sounded unpleasantly sarcastic. Martin grinned foolishly back.

The regular was about to wonder if this by any chance offered an opening for some kind of fight, when the door of the bar opened with a crash. Martin spilled most of the rest of his drink–but this time, he wasn't the only one. In the doorway stood Christian. He had somehow managed to make his hair look even wilder. He had had another line in the car and his eyes, which quickly swivelled across the room, now bulged manically from their sockets. In the too-large, ancient suit he was undoubtedly the most freakish, otherworldly individual anyone there had ever seen. Martin began to be genuinely terrified, but no-one was noticing him now.

With ghastly confidence, Christian strode up to the bar.

"A pint of your best bitter," he said, slapping a half-crown onto the counter.

The barmaid, normally unflappable to the point of catatonia, regarded the historic coin with puzzlement.

"That'll be two pound thirty-five," she said.

"WHAT?" gasped Christian. "The last time I was here it was two bob."

A few of the older men looked at the youthful Christian, who despite his lifestyle didn't look much older than his thirty years, and started doing some mental arithmetic.

"Unless... unless..." said Christian, grasping his brow. He turned to the landlord, who was sidling up to the barmaid in case she needed protection from this dangerous lunatic. "Quick, man, what date is it?"

"Six o' December," said the man suspiciously.

"The year, man, the year!"

"Two thousand and two," he said, slowly.

Christian groaned. This coincided with the uncomfortably sudden feeling that he had had far too many drugs, so the clammy sweat and white face looked like genuine symptoms of panic.

"I might not be too late."

He leaned over urgently to the landlord. "Have there been any strange occurrences round here lately? Crop circles? Animals or people disappearing, that kind of thing?"

MARTIN REALIZED THAT CHRISTIAN WAS DOING HIS RAF WING COMMANDER IMPRESSION

"Crop circles?" said one.

"That were made by–"

"They're not all fakes, you know," said Christian.

Meanwhile, as the landlord considered whether Mrs Hadleigh-Brown's weekend fling with the dentist should count as a strange disappearance, Christian turned his unnaturally piercing gaze to Martin.

"You seen any unusual lights in the sky in the last day or so?"

Martin opened and closed his mouth a couple of times.

"I said, have you seen any unusual lights in the sky?"

"Well," Martin heard his own cracked voice saying, "now you mention it, I have."

"Bluish? In a group of three? Triangular formation?"

Martin felt, for a moment, like saying "no, they were entirely imaginary", but instead decided to nod. He even said "how did you..."

"Scouts," said Christian bitterly. "That gives us a very short time. Someone buy me a drink, my money's no good here. Has anyone got a map of the area?"

Martin, awed, produced his from the inside pocket of his overcoat.

"Splendid. Just a half, we don't have time for a pint. Now, look here." He spread out the map on the table. "Where are we?"

Three quavering index fingers, almost

involuntarily it seemed, pointed to the village.

"Gentlemen," said Christian after a cursory study, "elementary triangulation will lead you to notice that we are at the precise midpoint of these three ancient monuments. Here, here, and here."

Martin realized that Christian was doing his RAF Wing Commander impersonation, one of his favourites, and relaxed very slightly.

"Only they're not monuments. Ancient they are–but they're not monuments. Or not in the way we imagine. You know how old they are?"

The regulars, who, like all country dwellers who grow up in the vicinity of neolithic sites, don't give a damn about them (unless they own a gift shop nearby), shook their heads.

"Thousands, I 'eard," said one, uncertainly.

"Four thousand, two hundred, give or take a few years," said Christian, giving the local his "well spotted, that chap" look. "Which is just about the time it takes a fleet of ships travelling at three-quarter light speed to make the round trip from here to Aldebaran and back. A long stretch of time for us, you may say; but not if you are, for all practical purposes, immortal. And," he added darkly, "very, very hungry."

There was a complete silence in the bar. Martin wondered whether this was because this was the calm before an act of spectacular, violent humiliation about to be collectively perpetrated on his own friend, or whether everyone was simply stunned.

Christian drank his half in one gulp and slammed the glass firmly down.

"Now who, here, excepting your good self, sir–" here he made a courteous half-bow to the landlord–"is in a position of authority?"

While everyone examined their own importance, an elderly man who had once been a Conservative district councillor tentatively raised a hand. Everyone reluctantly murmured assent.

Christian looked delighted. "National Service?"

The man, who had in fact had flat feet, nodded in spite of himself.

"Just the fellow. Now listen," he said. "What I am about to say may sound completely unbelievable to you, and if you want to throw me out right now, do so. But all I can say is this: by your actions tonight, the very future of humanity may be in your hands."

"'Ere," said a beefy farm worker who hadn't been in a fight for days, "'oo are you?"

Christian turned on him a look of deep pity and regret.

"I'm afraid I can't quite tell you that right now. All I can say is that I'm as human as anyone else round this bar tonight."

Now he really is going to get thumped, thought Martin. But Christian hadn't finished speaking.

"You look pretty strong. Do you reckon you could lead a group of five men to this point here–" he jabbed a finger at the nearest gothic-script "Tumulus" he could see–"take cover, and wait for something to happen. You'll know what it is when you see it. Got any weapons? Shotgun? Air rifle, even crow scarers–anything that makes a bang will do. Spades, pitchforks, anything that can turn your hands to. They won't be expecting a fight. Now, you, sir," he said, turning to the elderly ex-councillor, "take a group to here." (Another jab at a National Trust site.) "Same plan. Can you all also rustle up, um, a fifty-pound bag of fertiliser, a car battery, a pair of starter leads, and some protective goggles? You–" now he took in the landlord–"set up an operations centre here. Have you got any way of communicating with each other? Radio sets, that kind of thing?"

"We got our mobiles, only they don't work so well down here."

"Mobiles?" asked Christian, puzzled.

"Mobile phones," clarified one.

"Ah!" Christian beamed beatifically. "Of course! Can I see?"

He was handed a smart little silver set, turned it over, looked down its length, flipped it open and shut. "Charming. Quite primitive, but they'll do. Microwave technology, narrow band, I see. And the reason they don't work so well is that they're interfered with by the navigation beacons. The stones," he added, off-handedly, passing the phone back to its owner. "But that's all the better. You'll find–" he raised his eyebrows conspiratorially–"the interference works both ways."

"What about you?" asked a retired estate agent.

"I will be going here," said Christian, pointing to the third point on his essentially random triangle. "You with the map, you're with me. When did you see those lights?"

"I don't know... about six-thirty?" said Martin, wondering if it was the right answer.

Christian looked at the clock behind the bar and frowned. "As long as they are the scout ships, then that gives us less than an hour. Now you, landlord, have you got a pencil and paper? Yes? Excellent. Now," he said, lowering his voice to a murmur, "if I'm not back here by twelve, I want you to call this number in London–" he scribbled down Martin's sister's number–"and ask to be put in touch with whoever's in charge of Operation Sheep-dip. They'll see you get through. Don't take no for an answer–the file's obviously been dormant for at least thirty years. Come!" And, taking Martin by the elbow, he swept out of the pub.

"But what are we looking for?" asked the retired estate agent plaintively.

"You'll know when you see it!" shouted Christian. "Be alert! And watch the sheep!" Martin decided that he had now had enough of the countryside for a while, and that, on the whole, London would be a less stressful place to continue with his work. On the rather hurried drive up, he wondered aloud whether the villagers would have actually hung around waiting for ravenous aliens or suspicious sheep.

"Can't say I'm concerned one way or the other," said Christian. "The main thing is that they've been given a sense of purpose, we've had some fun, and you're getting a lift back to town. And the next time you're crazy enough to go down there again, you can explain your sudden absence by saying you were anally probed or something. You might even get a drink out of it. Some ointment, at the very least. They'll be delighted to see you. There are so few opportunities for country folk to go roaming around the countryside with flaming torches that they'll be grateful for the rest of their lives."

He never returned to the village, and shortly afterwards his sister sold the cottage so her children's school fees could be paid. But he did, at one interminable family bash, overhear his brother-in-law saying he was glad to be shot of the place, complaining about being pestered, once even in the middle of the night, by a man from the local pub asking anxiously about sheep-dip.

CLOSED

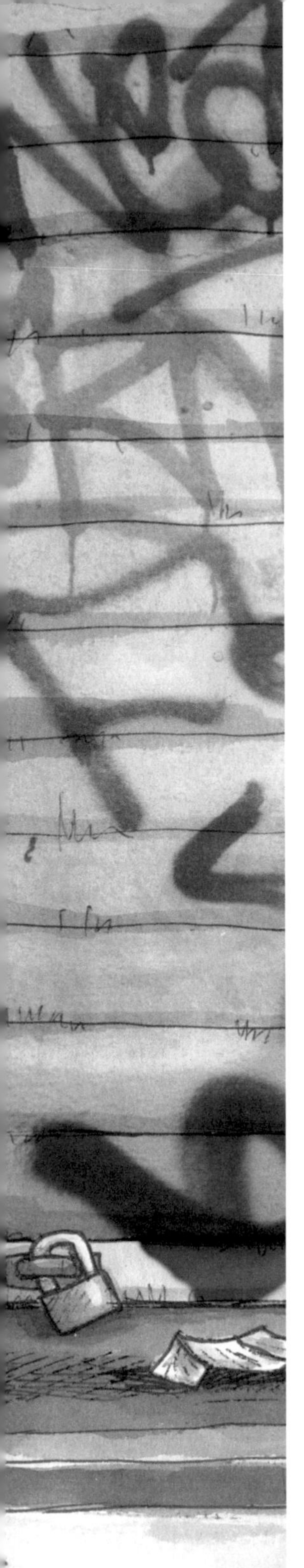

In Praise of Simple Pleasures

WILL GEORGE FIND TRUTH?
BY R.J. GHORBANI
ILLUSTRATION BY EDWIN MARNEY

On the third Monday of the longest January in living memory, George Bell lowered his head over the paper folds of his vinegar inhalation and sucked urgently at its healing vapours. Sitting on the concrete step of a disused shop, he wondered whether this sensation could be preserved somehow, perhaps by storing the papers in a vacuum jar to be revisited later, but concluded that its medicinal value lay in the warm potato poultice beneath. Resolving to let the smell linger on his fingers for as long as possible, he plunged them deep into the scalding, slimy solids. Of course, rationally, George knew that any effect on his health was likely to be a detrimental one and had felt his internal organs complain as he placed his order with the gargantuan woman at the greasy counter, unsure whether her presence should be taken as a testimony to the quality of the food or as a means to alleviate his guilt. But, he had been looking forward to this moment since the sun set over his milk and two sugars earlier that afternoon and he was determined to relish it. Tonight he had an extra need of the secure feeling that each mouthful gave him, as it slithered down his gullet in a wave of

> "WAS IT YOU WHO SENT THOSE IDIOTS ROUND TO MY FLAT?" SHE DEMANDED

malted euphoria and lay in wait for the survival situation that never came.

Hunched in his anorak, Georgie Porgie Ding Dong Bell could have been mistaken for an oversized school boy and, while he had never grown out of his puppy fat, he had gradually grown into everyone's expectations of him. He had married the first girl he kissed who didn't cry–Marjorie Raymond, or May as everyone called her (oh yes, he could almost hear them laughing, May Ray and Ding Dong), would be cooking for him in their modest bungalow as he ate–and he had slipped into a job with the city council to bide his time until retirement. Every day, for nigh on thirty years, he had traipsed between house, bus stop, office, without complaint, measuring his years of service in the bevelled heels of his shoes.

George could feel that it was around 5.30, which put less than an hour between him and the young woman, and gave him another half hour before May would begin to worry. He needed to think, to compose himself before he made his way home. The indignance that had refused to accompany him as he fled the featureless office had been usurped by a curiosity that forced him to process the encounter.

Visitors were not welcome on the seventeenth floor, a fact attested to by the lack of signage for Debt Management in the stairwell. But, the young woman had found her way there somehow and George had cursed the lack of security in the building as a shadow was cast over his department. In anticipation of the fried treat of home time, he had volunteered for an early tea break and was presiding over an empty office when she entered.

The speed and confidence of the footfalls that advanced across the grey cord carpet caused George to look up sooner than his studied indifference normally allowed. The feminine face, encircled by a halo of fake fur, surprised him pleasantly and he ventured a tight-lipped smile. Without pause or introduction, a woman the age of the daughter that he and May never had, pulled a crumpled A4 sheet from her pocket and demanded: "Was it you who sent those idiots round to my flat?" in an accent that was not local. Squinting, George recognised the outline of standard bailiff notification B52 and a signature that indisputably matched the name plate on his desk. Registering this connection in lieu of an answer, she raged: "Well, I hope you're satisfied; they've taken all my stuff."

George could feel the expletives caged behind her teeth and opened his mouth to explain that her possessions would be sold for a fair price to recover her debts. The Ms. Beckett of his letter, who refused to remain confined to paper, challenged "Listen, I don't mind paying for nurseries when I don't have any kids, or for hospitals that tell me I have to wait forty four weeks to be seen, or even for the people who have strewn rubbish all over the garden. What I do object to is you telling me I have to pay this much, on demand, when I don't have a regular income. I object to you refusing to take my calls and never phoning back when I leave endless messages and I object to you refusing to answer any of the letters I sent you explaining the situation." At this, she pulled out a ream of typewritten sheets and sprinkled them liberally over his desk, demanding "So, what are you going to do about it?"

It was then that George ventured to speak, ploughing his limited resources for appropriate platitudes. "I'm afraid there's nothing I can do, Ms. Beckett. Once the bailiffs have seiz... have taken your possessions, it's out of my hands."

"Well, you're just going to have to get it back into your hands. I want you to phone them now, tell them there has been a mistake and order them to bring back my things. Then I want you to write me a letter, on headed paper, that gives me more time to pay these jumped up charges of yours."

The defiance of Alice Beckett's stare belied nothing of the tears that waited for her anger to subside. When George flatly refused, she scanned the department for a higher authority and he was relieved that his colleagues had deserted him, imagining the shame of undergoing this ordeal in front of those for whom he felt no affinity.

Sensing that their confrontation was approaching its end, George relinquished the name of his superior when it was requested and watched as she wrote it awkwardly on the back of his letter, using the palm of her hand as a surface against which to press her ballpoint. Finally, lowering her voice somewhat menacingly, she asked: "Do you get some kind of perverse pleasure, sending thugs round to intimidate young women?" If George had any insight into the workings of the persona who confronted him, he would have known that she had hesitated to invoke this point, believing the injustice she had suffered to be deeper than gender. Turning to leave, she muttered "pathetic" under her breath.

When the heavy door of the department swung shut, George sighed and, when his colleagues filed in merrily to while away the afternoon, he darted through the door by which they had re-entered to calm his stomach in the staff toilet. But, his concentration was disrupted and the payment schedules he had been drafting for the pensioners in Maxwell Drive would have to wait until the morning, he thought as he shuffled back around his desk. On the stroke of five, he pulled on his rustling coat and eased his way innocuously out of the room. Even as he pressed the lift arrow on the landing and charted its laborious ascendance through the illuminated numbers, George struggled to clear his mind of earlier events and, when it stopped at the floor below, interrupting the flow of his descent, he expressed his annoyance in a loud tut.

Momentarily blinded by the fug of his day, he failed to recognise the fur collar of the person who entered on the sixteenth floor until she turned to confront him with a changed face. She waited a moment, registering his passive distaste and, in a calm voice that spoke of diffused rage, asked:

"Just what is it that makes you tick, Mr. Bell?"

"What do you mean?" he responded, prompting a prepared answer that was difficult to decode:

"I mean, I came to you today as a human being you had never met before.

The Germ Organization Presents

JOHN MOORE HALF AWAKE

Available now from
www.halfawake.co.uk
www.johnmoore23.co.uk
and discerning record shops everywhere

Someone else might have tried to help me and I was wondering why you didn't."

"Well, you didn't give me much of a chance, striding into my office, guns blazing."

"But, be honest. Even if I had come to you meekly, you wouldn't have helped me would you?"

"I might have," George dissembled.

"We both know that's not true. But could you have done something if you had wanted to?"

For a moment, George weighed up the wisdom of honesty in this situation as the lift creaked agonisingly downwards. Instinct cautioned him against truth but he found himself saying:

"Well, I suppose I could have tried to reason with the bailiffs."

"And you didn't because...?"

"Primarily because of the amount of work that this would entail," he replied, the formality of language remaining his last bastion of defence in a confined space.

"What? A phone call? A letter?"

"And all the paperwork for my superiors."

"What kind of a system is it that prevents people from helping each other?" she asked rhetorically, "Don't you ever want to change it?"

"I did." He confided, with the emphasis on the past tense.

"Let me guess," said Alice, an edge of cruelty creeping into her words. "You have been in this job since you left school, it's the only thing you know how to do. In the beginning, you thought you would change the world but then the system got the better of you? I don't believe that you ever tried to change anything, George. You just accepted life

"WHAT WOULD HAPPEN IF EVERYONE WAS LIKE YOU, GEORGE?"

the way it is, didn't you?" Her words reverberated around the steel capsule and ricocheted against his rigid body. "Haven't you ever needed help?"

In reaching for a convincing denial, proud of his self-sufficiency, he found his times of need flickering reluctantly across his mind. He remembered his mother's protracted illness and the care she had received and was visited by the image of his car in a snowdrift and the kindness of the strangers who had taken him in.

As the lift clunked to a halt at the bottom of its shaft, she asked "What would happen if everyone was like you, George?" and disappeared into the night, leaving him blinking in the lurid veneer of reception.

Half an hour closer to home, eyes watering in the vinegar vapours, George considered his position in the scheme of things and a sense of worthlessness seeped up from the cold step. He thought of the world without co-operation that he had worked so hard to create and was ashamed. For a moment, he toyed with the idea of running away, of turning his back on predictability with a dramatic last act. But the burden of knowledge weighed down a body unfit for the purpose. As he picked at the last flecks of potato that had fused with the paper, he resolved to do things differently, grateful for the glimpse of humanity from which he had protected himself for so long.

THE PRACTICAL IDLER

THE PRACTICAL IDLER

Welcome to the Practical Idler. This season, we suggest various ways of enjoying yourself, including tractor rides and going to see the Alabama 3. Graham Burnett introduces his new gardening column with an insight into the joys and wonders of the permaculture system. We offer hints and tips on the mystical art of hitching from a past master. In our books section, we meet the incomparable George Macdonald Fraser, author of the *Flashman* books, and in the Idler Abroad, Clare Dowdy reports back from Tanzania. Chris Yates continues his tea column and Greg Rowland rounds things off.

YOUR GUIDE TO THE EASY LIFE

STATIONERY REVIEW:

MOLESKINE SLIMLINES

Tom Hodgkinson likes the squashiness

We're always searching for the perfect notebook, and regular readers will know that we have in the past favoured the Moleskine. However, our objection to the thick, hardback, traditional Moleskine is that it's just a little too bulky to fit in a back pocket. That's why we were so thrilled to discover that Moleskine have produced a new set of thin notebooks, nicely bendy and squashy, but still with the distinctive pleasing elegance of the original. They are selling three of these little notebooks in pack for £4.50, and seem to have sorted out wonderful distribution, the things being available in ordinary bookshops like Books Etc. The covers are black card, the back pages are perforated for ripping out and giving your phone number or the title of a book to friends and strangers, and the notebooks also feature a handy little pocket. In addition, the pack comes with a little if rather mystifying set of stickers with letters on them. Very handy, very lovely, with these unpretentious notebooks you can write down your innermost thoughts and the shopping list side by side. They also look quite nice when put away next to each other on a bookshelf, providing an archive of your life, in all its domestic, reflective and practical variety.

THE SMALLER, LESS INTIMIDATING MOLESKINE

THE ANGLER:

FILTHY LUCRE

Kevin Parr is happy with old stuff

I know a carp fisherman. He is very much an acquaintance, but we share an interest in angling and always chat when our paths cross.

Every year, around March, Jim trades in his matching trio of hi-tech rods and reels for the latest versions, hot off the far-Eastern production lines, carbon fibres still glowing.

There was nothing wrong with Jim's old rods, of course, except that they were a year out of date, old hat, and, besides, he was going to be the talk of the bankside with his new weaponry.

Not, however, that Jim's rods actually see much action. He rarely ventures out onto the bank, but instead speaks of past glories and complains of the state of his local lake.

"It's a disgrace—overgrown, weedy, you can't even see the water in some swims," he complains.

"It sounds perfect to me," I argue.

But Jim needs trimmed and manicured vegetation. A nice man-made platform jutting into the lake on which he can assemble his arsenal without getting mud on his Nike trainers.

It is clear why Jim is not someone I care for particularly, and certainly not someone I would wish to share bank space with, though I encounter others of his ilk with increasing regularity.

Angling has become a place of fashion and image. It is no longer important whether you catch fish or not, if you look the part then you gain respect. What a sorry world, and how sad that so many fisherfolk are naïve enough to be exploited into paying over the odds for equipment they simply do not need.

Take the bobbin, for example.

This is a simple device which hangs on the line between the reel and first rod ring, which allows a biting fish to take the bait with little resistance, but gives the angler a visual indication of the take.

I tend to use a washing-up bottle top, or some folded tin-foil, or, a little forked twig, or even a piece of lightly squeezed bread.

For the image conscious, however, bobbins are available in chrome or plated silver; with interchangeable screw-in brass weights to counter changes in wind-speed, and even, I kid you not, hand-painted in the colours of your favourite football team.

The big craze currently sweeping the fishing world, however, is "Camou".

Camouflage is the new black. Coats, trousers, hats and boots—your average angler looks like a commando skulking down the river bank, and boy are the tackle manufacturers cashing in. You can buy camou brollies, camou gloves, camou sleeping bags and camou chairs. You can even buy camouflage sellotape to wrap around every inch of tackle item that doesn't already "blend naturally into the background".

However, to avoid accusations of hypocrisy, I should now admit to possessing a "camou" jacket myself. I was chatting to a friend back in January, when he offered me a coat for free.

"I've been selling them," he said, "but no-one needs the extra-extra large ones so you can have one—should fit you perfectly."

What I fear most about wearing this coat is the way I look. One should never feel self conscious when fishing, and suddenly I am. I feel as though I'm walking down the street with shades on my head, an FCUK T-shirt, and one of those hairstyles that we used to call mullets.

Still, at least I can relax with the fact that I didn't pay 150 quid for it; which brings me back to Jim, and his compulsion to spend as much money as possible on his fishing tackle.

A fishing rod, if reasonably looked after, can last a lifetime. There is simply no need to change it annually, and, what is perhaps more important, is the role a rod actually takes in the catching of fish.

It is not simply a levering tool, or a casting implement, it is an extension of the forearm—a part of you. After a few years of using the same rod one begins to forget it is even there. It is as though one's wrist has grown by twelve feet, mending the line and tweaking a bait as easily as if using one's fingers.

Stephen Hendry, the seven time snooker champion used the same cue for his whole career before it was stolen and his form capitulated.

Whereas Ted Hankey, former

JOE HARRISON

world darts champion, has thrown the same arrows for so long that his fingers have worn away the metal shaft—they now weigh half their original weight and when asked to throw with a modern day equivalent, he struggled to get a single treble.

And so it is with the angler.

Your tackle is what you use to think in the water, to understand the currents and undulations. To replace a component is to dilute its' efficiency.

My point could be proved by a young lad fishing a nondescript and previously unheard of little pool in Oxfordshire. Using the crudest of tackle, aimed at the numerous suicidal small carp in the pond, he caught the biggest perch ever.

The specimen angling world was in disbelief.

And the loveliest postscript to his capture is the fact that though countless people have approached the pool with every modern method known to man, that perch has evaded recapture, and, in fact, has almost certainly now died of old age.

So a young lad from Oxford has his name forever etched in angling folklore, and even in the twenty-first century, a fisherman's tale might just be true.

TEA TIME:

A TEA DRINKER'S DIARY

by Chris Yates

TUESDAY

John. G., a good friend of mine who, two years ago, moved to North Carolina, came to visit today and tell me about life among the god-fearers of the USA. The cultural life was, he said, surprisingly good, the people were interesting—especially the women, but you couldn't get a good cup of tea—a really good cup of tea—anywhere. We sat in my garden drinking Ridgeways Organically Grown Tea. The late afternoon sky was intensely blue, the hay had just been cut on the other side of the valley and the air smelt like a barn at harvest time. John eventually stopped talking about America. Three minutes is a long silence in his company.

"Tell me the name of this tea again?" he asked, and after I'd replied there was another long pause, and then he said: "I think I'm going to move back to England."

WEDNESDAY

At last! I've found a tea cup to replace the old favourite that I smashed last year. Since then I've been drinking from an odd assortment of vessels, all of them perfectly serviceable, but none quite as good as the well-tarnished China bucket that had become part of my anatomy over these last ten years.

I don't like a shallow bowl that palms the tea and I don't like a tall narrow tower that tubes it. I want a cup that comfortably cups. I don't want a rim that's too delicate and precious, but nor do I wish for one like the rim of a flowerpot. Today I found a cup named after a flower—Rose of England—but the rim is just right and though it's bone china it's not prissy and it holds a satisfactory half a pint. Already I can feel it growing into my right hand.

THURSDAY

Received the summer edition of *Teapot Times*, edited by Paul Machin, who, in his editorial, writes that the consumption of economy tea in Britain is declining while sales of herbal, organic and Fairtrade teas are increasing. There is a fascinating feature in the evolution of the teapot, with photographs of eccentric contemporary designs, all of which would make great conversation stoppers at a tea party. There are reassuring medical surveys showing that tea prevents everything from prostate cancer to tooth decay and a guide to the world's best tea rooms, from the Ritz Hotel in London to the Plantation Hotel in Sri Lanka, where you can drink your tea looking out over the green Kelami valley where *The Bridge Over the River Qwai* was shot.

Clipper produce some superb teas but they should also be congratulated for producing this quirky and informative little journal.

FRIDAY

Another weird coincidence. Yesterday I was reading about the tea-producing Kelami Valley in

WILL YATES

Teapot Times, and today I was given a packet of unblended broken orange pekoe which comes direct from Kelami valley Plantations Limited, Sri Lanka.

But when this packet is finished, I don't think I'll be able to drink another cup of tea—ever—at least not unless I can go back and get some more of this miracle leaf from "The cool misty reaches of Nuwara Eliya—home of the finest quality tea in the world". There is something appropriate about the name of it—"Lover's Leap". You drink it, you understand that nothing can ever be as good again. You throw yourself off a precipice.

The reason it's so good is that it's so fresh—it was probably packed in Sri Lanka only a few days ago and a friend bought it as a present for me when she visited the plantation. So even if I tracked down a supplier in England, the tea wouldn't have the perfect, astonishing radiance of this particular sample. It is brewing in an old brown china teapot on the windowsill next to me. And now I shall take a sip from my new cup. O gods! It's divine! My friend John G. might be moving back to England, but I might be gone by the time he gets here, having moved east, to the Kelami Valley.

SATURDAY

Edward Barder, who makes exquisite split cane fishing rods, came to see me and tell me how he had not been catching trout on the local chalk stream. After a really absurd fishing story about a canal towpath, a speeding cyclist who looked like Spiderman and an angler who didn't look behind him when he cast, I wiped the tears from my eyes and said "would you like a cup of tea?"

I made him a pot of L.L. He was treated to a taste of heaven and the only words he uttered for the rest of the afternoon were: "Do you think we could have just one more pot?"

So it was a tragic day in the end. There's only a spoonful of the luxurious leaves left.

THE PASSENGER:

MAKE HAY WHILE THE SUN SHINES

Fanny Johnstone on the tractor. Illustration by Aaron Plowdle

People are always listing the 100 things we should do before we die. This is irritating and arrogant. Why presume that climbing Kilimanjaro is any more interesting or rewarding than sinking two bottles of wine and smoking roll-ups while you watch swallows build this year's nest? Why should visiting the Vatican be more spiritually uplifting than a hay bale ride on a tractor through country lanes? If I was the kind of person who wrote those petty lists I know which one I'd recommend. But it's an obvious choice anyway because you can't roll a fag on a mountaintop and you can't smoke in the Vatican.

I spent a lot of my '70s childhood sitting on a John Deer tractor. On a whim my father had recently become a farmer so the tractor was a tool of the trade it was "essential" for me to learn how to use. The fact that it was lame and rusting in the home field of our 13 acre Cornish small-holding made no difference to me. Along with wretched sheep, disused pig-stys and a violent rooster called Rupert who flew at me sideways every time I crossed the farmyard, we inherited the tractor when we bought the farm.

Sitting on the edge of that bull-head seat with my hands gripped around the rusting steering wheel, and my feet reaching for pedals, I found a starting point for fantastic adventures. Together the tractor and I searched the world. We rescued slaves from the salt mines in Siberia, we won prizes at country fairs, and in the drought of 1976 we brought ice-cream to the sad hot people of London town. We returned, from all our adventures, as heroes.

Although we were self-sufficient (my parents the rural parallel of Tom and Barbara Good in *The Good Life*) we had another tractor which worked. In about 1975 my father bought a 1947 light tractor for £50. It was a Massey Ferguson TVO. TVO stands for Tractor Vaporising Oil which meant that you started the tractor on petrol but then switched to TVO which was much cheaper. This was convenient because, at this point, we had little or no money.

(To give you an example let me tell you that the sweaters I wore were made from the wool sheared from our sheep, which was spun by my mother on a spinning-wheel, and dyed with the lichen which we picked from rocks on the beach. The sweaters were then knitted by my mother, worn by my brother and then given to me when he had out grown them. So you see

I REMEMBER BEING SO PROUD THAT I COULD PICK A HAY BALE UP WITH MY LITTLE FINGER. BUT NOW IT MAKES ME SOUND TERRIFYING

a dead tractor was a pretty exciting toy in those days.)

Our tractor pulled the trailer my father had fixed, and as our neighbours were real Cornish farmers all of us would help to bring in each other's hay. At sunrise we set out to the fields, and throughout the day we'd heave hay bales (which were small and rectangular then) up onto the trailer. I remember being so proud that I could pick a hay bale up with my little finger. But now it makes me sound terrifying and explains why, when we played "it" at school I paffed those Cornish kids across the other side of the playground without meaning to.

Back in the fields we ate pasties for lunch (probably) and rounded off the day with homebrewed beer or elderflower wine (true). But first was clambering up the comparativley high tower of hay bales for the ride home. The excitement for us kids was almost unbearable. Some would kneel boldly upright to survey the passing panoramas while others would lie flat on top. Our fingers gripped the bailer twine to keep us held tight to the load which itself was not strapped to the trailer at all but somehow, miraculously, stayed in its neat high-rise Rubick's cube formation. One of the kids from down the lan, did fall off into a hedge once, but she bounced right back with a bloody nose and bruised knees and was hauled, at her request, back up to the top again.

As well as helping to run the farm the tractor came in use when our car wouldn't start. This was pretty often. Fortunately we lived at the top of a hill so we could bump start the car all the way down the road towards Lowertown. When, in the valley, the car still hadn't started my mother would call Pa from the public telephone box that stood by the river. My father would then trundle down on the tractor and pull the car all the way back up to start the process all over again.

At the other end of the country a friend of mine, called Jaime Turner, was growing up having tractor races on the beaches of South Uist in the Outer Hebrides. These were also on Massey Fergusons. And now Jaime's cousin, Ali Macaskill, (a lookout man for the MoD on Uist for years) has just made his fortune with another cousin, Duncan-John, by renting out their services to bring in all the island's hay. With brand new tractors it only needs the two cousins, and the bales are huge so no-one gets to sit on the trailer at the end of a day's baling. This is sad because it means none of the kids on Uist will know what it's like to climb up to the top of the dusty hay bales and lord it over their own, deleriously bleak but beautiful countryside.

So, while not wanting to be an arrogant, annoying person who recommends Things You Should Do Before You Die, if you can find a farm that will allow you to ride a tractor, to help with old-fashioned hay baling sessions and to round it all off with a hay bail ride then do it. All of you will remember the smell of new hay, and the dust on your legs and the evening's first glug of beer or lemonade forever. And afterwards you can open a bottle of wine, light a cigarette and watch the new baby swallows learn how to fly.

IDLE PURSUITS:

GET OUT ON THE HIGHWAY

Ash Prosser with a hitchhiker's guide. Illustration by Andy Council

These days, with the likes of Megabus and their too-low intercity fares pricing some hitchhikers into the public transport market and off the roadsides, the money-conscious (and indeed money-free) hitcher has all the more reason to get out onto the verges and protect the dying art of hitching. Sure I can travel from my home in Devon to London for a fiver on some crappy old double-decker, but what kind of story is it to tell on arrival that you got on a bus and then five hours later got to London? If you want adventure and interesting stories, then you have to hitch. Additionally, with the interesting people you meet while hitching, there's always the possibility of doors opening. When was the last time you got a job from a bus ride? I was hitching to London the other day, got a lift from the editor of this magazine and got the job of writing this piece, so it just goes to show.

Riding free across the country in other people's cars, vans, dormobiles, people carriers, trucks and coaches, at their expense, is as rewarding an experience for the hitcher's karmic accounts as it is for the bank balance. Hitching is a supreme test of the old magician's maxim, "positive thoughts bring positive things, negative thoughts bring negative things" and rewards those of sunny disposition, the unattached, and the patient in equal measure.

Indeed, the roadside is a marvellous place to learn about the tricks of the magical trade. On more than one occasion, after too long a wait in one place, I have sung mantras for Ganesha, the Hindu God of Obstacle Removal, and had a car pick me up with a statue of the same elephant-headed deity glued to the dashboard. Once, on a rainy stretch of impossibly fast road, after an hour in one place, and with the clock ticking on my appointment time, I sang Blake's *Jerusalem*, and, sure enough, my old biology teacher turned up with the Under-14s rugby team on tour in the area in a minibus, with the school motto *Dat Deus Incrementum* (God Gives Us Strength) emblazoned on the side. All those years of singing the old public school favourite in assembly had finally paid off.

A test of the karmic validity of where you are going and what you are doing is measured by the barometer of how easily you get the lift. If, as has happened to me, the car pulls up as you are drawing your invocatory star in the earth about you with your magic wand, then you know you are going to the right place. Sometimes, the wait is a test of

HELL'1

your powers of concentration. I once had to chant non-stop for an hour in plummeting temperatures while hitching at night inside the Finnish Arctic Circle before finally getting a lift with a tour bus. Desperation is often the mother of conjuration.

The hitcher must have a supreme level of self-confidence and absolutely *know* that he will reach his destination, otherwise he is simply a fool standing on the side of the road with his thumb hanging in the air. I myself ran foul of this rule when trying to hitch back to a hostel in Snowdonia in worsening weather conditions, after coming down off a mountain too late in the day. With just a handful of cars passing me after an hour's waiting, I despaired of getting a lift, so went to ask for help from a nearby farmhouse. While the kind farmer was running me back, we were followed all the way home by someone else who lived with me at the hostel, and who would have picked me up about five minutes after I abandoned the hitch. You must *see* in your mind's eye your arrival at your destination, and it surely *will* occur.

Faith is the key to the successful hitch. In an age of *Crimewatch*, many are afraid to hitch because they believe they will be picked up by a nut. Similarly, many will not pick up a hitcher because they believe them to be a nut. I, when hitching, and knowing myself to be fine, and in no way a nut, send out only for someone fine, and in no way a nut, to pick me up. Very occasionally, it is possible to sail very close to the wind during such tests of faith. On the way to Glastonbury one day, one fatigue-clad Liverpudlian, can of beer nestling between his knees, picked me up and scared the living shit out of me. He said that if the "busies" picked us up they'd think we were terrorists and invited me to look in the back of the car in some bag he had. When I saw the set of guns I wondered finally if this was the nightmare lift that all hitchers fear, until I realised the guns were paintball guns and that the driver, like his passenger, was a magical player in the game of life. "It's psychic warfare out there every day, mate," he told me. To get him off that subject, I

THE HITCHER MUST HAVE A SUPREME LEVEL OF SELF-CONFIDENCE

pointed out his little Ozzy Osbourne figurine on his dash, and we missed my turning while singing Black Sabbath songs in tribute to the great man who had come off his quad bike earlier in the week.

There is nothing like hitching for heaven and hell. One minute you are standing on the side of the road, freezing, in total despair, wondering what the hell you are doing, and the next you are in some open-topped sports car, still freezing, but zooming along at a 100mph, mad driver's spliff in hand, wondering what the hell you are doing. It can go either way.

And it's great if you are on the holy man ticket. Numerous times I get in the car, let people tell me their whole life story, straighten 'em out with pertinent observations, they make their mind up about the next phase of their life, I get to where I am going, and everyone gets what they deserve.

THE BROWSER:

BERNADINE EVARISTO

Karen Hooper has a chat with the young novelist

EVARISTO: DON'T PUT HER IN A BOX

Bernadine Evaristo's latest novel *Soul Tourists* goes on the road with Stanley and Jessie, two modern day characters escaping the routine of their boring lives. But the journey takes on a whole new meaning when Stanley encounters ghosts of colour from Europe's dusty archives. The novel builds on Evaristo's much acclaimed novels-in-verse *Lara* (1997), a partly autobiographical work that took her to Nigeria and Brazil and *The Emperor's Babe* (2001) an extravaganza set in Roman Londinium.

"I THOUGHT, WHY NOT MAKE LONDON SOMETHIG OF THE MULTI-RACIAL MELTING POT THAT WAS ROME?"

IDLER: Have you ever had the chance to be idle?

BERNADINE EVARISTO: I once spent a year being completely idle. I camped by a lagoon in Turkey and did nothing but eat, sleep and swim. It was my belated gap year and if I could do it again I would because by the time I returned to London I'd made some dramatic life changes. Making a proper commitment to writing was one.

IDLER: The novel encompasses poetry and all sorts of literary devices. How did this form evolve?

EVARISTO: I wasn't planning on it being so experimental, but when I wrote it as a straightforward prose novel it just didn't work; then I started experimenting with the original manuscript and different forms started to emerge; the poetry, prose, prose poetry, script, budgets, a death certificate, a Q&A device, divorce documents, yes, all sorts of madness! There's a lot of theatre in my work and I realise it's because I trained as an actress and originally wrote for theatre. My natural voice is poetic and I cannot avoid that. I should stop trying to conform.

IDLER: *The Emperor's Babe* is fascinating in that it explodes the myth that there wasn't a black presence in Britain until the 1948 Windrush influx. You take the reader to a very multi-cultural Roman Londinium. Where did that come from?

EVARISTO: I was Poet In Residence at The Museum of London in 1999—that was excellent for research, but not particularly helpful in discovering multi-cultural Londinium as almost no research has been done in this area. I worked with the premise that the Roman Empire stretched over 9,000 kms into Africa and Asia; there were lots of good roads and travelling across the Empire, so I thought why not make London something of the multi-racial melting pot that was Rome? As we know there were black soldiers in the Roman army at Hadrian's Wall in the early 3rd century, I thought, why not London too? The museum now has a black Roman character played by an actor who guides people around the Roman part of the museum. I get great satisfaction from that very tangible result.

IDLER: How did you get from *The Emperor's Babe* to *Soul Tourists*?

EVARISTO: I'm interested in writing fiction, which conflates the historical with the contemporary, as well as writing about relationships, which is the stuff of our daily lives. The *Emperor's Babe* might be set in the past, but it has modern day allusions. *Soul Tourists* started as a story about the Jessie and Stanley characters travelling across Europe in a car and the imbalanced power dynamic between them. But I couldn't just write a road movie, it needed to be a bigger book, so I inserted the historical ghosts, which I felt gave the story a new gravitas.

IDLER: So do Jessie and Stanley need an explanation about who they are historically? *Soul Tourists* begins with the death of Stanley's father, who is Afro-Caribbean... is this the end of postcolonial thinking; celebrating that generation but saying, now we move on?

EVARISTO: That's an interesting reading of it but when I'm writing I'm not consciously addressing critical theories. I can't wear an academic hat as well as a creative one. What I think is important to us black people in Britain or Europe is that if we want to live here we have to put down roots, as we have done, and while our histories may be informed by a post-colonial reality, our contemporary presence cannot be so easily defined. I believe that there are connections to be made with black European history that we haven't yet explored—and this is what interested me with this novel. The ghosts, in one sense, show Stanley that European history has broader and deeper African/Black connections than he realised—which really excites him. The ghosts also act as his spiritual helpers on his adventure across Europe and into self-discovery.

IDLER: I know the ghosts had to fit into a geographical journey but how did you choose this wonderful Shakespearian/carnivalesque parade?

EVARISTO: These are characters I'd read about whom I just thought were fascinating—like the Chevalier de St George—he now has a street named after him in Paris, He was a major 18th Century figure in France who then completely disappeared from history until very recently. Pushkin is considered the father of Russian literature and his great grandfather was Ethiopian, Major General Ibrahim Gannibal. When I was in Russia I saw statues of him everywhere. But when I mentioned his ancestry to Russians, they laughed at me and dismissed the very idea as preposterous or they said it was "rumoured" that he had some Arab blood. As the novel travels through Turkey, where his great grandfather was enslaved, it seemed opportune to slot Pushkin in there.

It's quite hard to locate many black female historical figures. Lucy Negro was a real 16th Century courtesan and in the novel I turn her into Shakespeare's dark lady of the sonnets. Despite all the arguments about the identity of the "dark lady", as a writer I give myself license to play with such images. It was much fun to do. Louise-Marie was the illegitimate daughter of Queen Marie-Therese, wife of Louis XIV. It was rumoured that her father was Nabo, a black dwarf from Dahomey. I like debunking the myths that abound about racial purity, especially in the upper echelons of our societies. I like being irreverent.

IDLER: You have an incredible imagination; what fires it?

EVARISTO: Have I? Maybe it's just that mine is unleashed. I guess it's like any other muscle, the more you use it the stronger it becomes. The bottom line is that I like to do things differently. I have a stubbornness which I've inherited from both my parents which has mutated into finding my own way of seeing and interpreting the world. A bloody-mindedness. I select my influences quite carefully. I won't read many books *du jour* because I don't want to subconsciously assimilate the critically successful stories and styles of my contemporaries, and lose my own original edge as a result. I do buy a lot of contemporary fiction, but it might take many years before I read them. I never want my work to be considered derivative, although it's a marketing tag, which sells books.

IDLER: You say you do not consider yourself a post-colonial writer and yet you use Oscar Wilde's statement, "The one duty we owe to history is to rewrite it", as an epigraph to *The Emperor's Babe*. Do you not see your work as "writing back" to the empire?

EVARISTO: I don't know of any writer who welcomes reductive labelling of any kind whether it is "woman writer", "black writer" or "working class writer". It seems to me that the only writers who avoid such labelling are white, male, heterosexual and not working class. They are called writers, full stop. Oh what a privilege. So you see, yes, I do object to being called a post-colonial writer. I am a writer, full stop. However, I am aware that in the academy I have to fall under the umbrella of some theory or other, and in some cases this is the postcolonial box in others it is the black British box. *The Emperor's Babe*, and so too *Lara*, can be read very broadly. They can also be taught across the boundaries of historical fiction/postmodern fiction/genre-busting fiction/contemporary poetry - many things. I am British, born and raised, exploring areas of personal interest, some of which can be sourced back to my heritage, which is multiple.

IDLER: Who has inspired you?

EVARISTO: Derek Walcott. I love his *Midsummer* collection because it was my introduction to his poetry. How about this line: "The jet bores like silverfish through volumes of clouds." Or "Chicago's avenues, as white as Poland/A blizzard of heavenly coke hushes the ghetto". Isn't it just amazing? It blew my breath away. Morrison, Updike, Chamoiseau, Okri, Ishiguro, Marquez and Anne Michaels have also moved me. In my formative years Tennyson's *Le Morte d'Arthur*, Chaucer, *Under Milkwood*, by Dylan Thomas, and Greek drama, I still love *Electra* and *Antigone*.

"I LIKE DEBUNKING THE MYTHS THAT ABOUND ABOUT RACIAL PURITY... I LIKE BEING IRREVERENT"

IDLER: You take your reader on great journeys; where is Bernadine Evaristo next taking us?

EVARISTO: I'd rather not say until it's completed but just to drop a hint, it will be about a world turned upside down.

IDLER: You clearly work very hard writing—when do you do when you get the chance to relax?

EVARISTO: I have a wild social life.

THE BROWSER:

GEORGE MACDONALD FRASER

and Dan Kieran in conversation

Illustrations by Arthur Barbosa

Photography by Rachel Poulton

George Macdonald Fraser is a difficult man to interview. Literally. He lives in the depths of the Isle of Man, has no need to court publicity (when the press release on your latest book includes gushing quotes on your work from PG Wodehouse, Auberon Waugh, and Kingsley Amis it's a safe bet that whatever you write is going to be impressive) and at 80, you can forgive him for not wanting, in the words of Bill Hicks, "to plough through this shit one more time". But after a few polite refusals I managed to corner him during the press junket for *Flashman on the March*, the latest installment in the adventures of Sir Harry Flashman, V.C K.C.B K.C.I.E. Once settled, he immediately began quizzing me about *The Idler.*

GEORGE MACDONALD FRASER: So, tell me, is this Jerome's *Idler*?

IDLER: Well we're the third incarnation of Samuel Johnson's *Idler*. Jerome K Jerome edited the second of the three and I think all have had the same purpose. To celebrate the idea of being responsible for your own life, and not being bullied into a job and a life you can't stand.

GMF: That's marvellous. I never knew that, thank you for the copy, I'll read it with great interest.

IDLER: It was wonderful to read *Flashman* again, it's like listening to an old friend.

GMF: Well, that's very kind.

IDLER: I read that the only thing you share with him is that you both think in the same way.

GMF: That's right.

IDLER: It's a voice and a perspective that you don't hear often these days…

GMF: Well political correctness has made people frightened of the truth, there's no doubt about that. There's a great reluctance, for some reason or other, to tell the truth. Now Flashman, however he may have lied in his everyday life, no better than everyone else probably, nevertheless he's absolutely honest about himself. He knows what he is and he thinks he knows what the world is [laughs].

IDLER: But his sense of perspective must have come from you and your life experiences.

GMF: I suppose so, yes. I am a cynic and I tend to believe the worst in people. I take a very jaundiced view of international affairs and politics in general. I think the war in Iraq was a war crime. I think it was a disgrace and I'm horrified that Parliament allowed it. I'm still haunted by the image of Tony Blair in the American Senate trying to convince the world he's Churchill.

IDLER: In the Victorian era they were more up front about their motives for going to war…

GMF: In the introduction to this new book I've compared the Abysinnian war, and the straightforward honourable way that Britain went about it, and the dishonourable way that we've gone about this one. There's an awful lot of talk about the Victorians' hypocrisy but the Victorians weren't in the same league compared with today! People are now talking about the American Empire. It's not, I don't suppose, an Empire, not in the sense that ours was. For one thing ours was efficient and in my view, very beneficial. And I don't think theirs is going to be either.

IDLER: I came across a quote of yours where you said that you consider yourself forty years out of date and that's why living in the Isle Of Man is perfect for you.

GMF: It is behind the times. I think everyone on the Island will agree with that and they like it that way. It's much pleasanter. I'll be delighted to get back [laughing].

IDLER: Is this, doing publicity and interviews, the nearest you get to hard work in the sense of hard work being something you have to endure?

GMF: Oh yes, I know exactly what you mean. Writing is not hard work. At least I've never found it to be, but this, this is drudgery (laughing).

IDLER: I'm convinced that you're an Idler, have you ever given it much thought?

GMF: Well I don't think that even Jerome was an Idler.

IDLER: An Idler is anyone who does their own thing and refuses to be dictated too,

GMF: Well that's about right, that was probably Jerome's idea too because God knows he wasn't idle. Was it him who said, "I love my work and I take it down and dust it from time to time"?

IDLER: There is that famous quote "I love work, I could sit and look at it for hours".

GMF: Well that's probably the one [laughing].

IDLER: For us being idle is about having the time to think and be in control of your own time.

GMF: Well you can't help having great sympathy with that. I hate that we have such a materialistic society and that we're so debt-ridden, that really worries me. I loathe these ads on television, trying to get people to borrow more and more money. I mean whatever happened to the Protestant ethic?

"WRITING IS NOT HARD WORK, AT LEAST I'VE NEVER FOUND IT TO BE"

IDLER: The idea of saving for something seems so out of date now. Can we talk a bit about the role of your work in your life? You spent many years in the army, then you worked in the newspaper trade, after that you started writing *Flashman*, which led to a career in Hollywood as a screenwriter. Was that all an organised plan?

GMF: Well I wasn't going to be good for anything else when I came out of the army. I went into journalism and I loved it. As you probably know it's better than working [laughs]. It's terrific fun. My wife and I were both reporters, and we went to Canada as reporters after we got married. Then we came back and had the family, and then I just kept on going until I decided that I wanted to get out of newspapers.

IDLER: What was it that set you off on to a different path?

GMF: I was deputy Editor of the *Glasgow Herald* and they made me acting Editor when the Editor retired. But I understood that I probably wouldn't be made Editor and indeed I wasn't. So I went back to being Deputy and I thought, "I don't need twenty years of this!" [laughs]. You know! And apparently I said to my wife, "I'm going to write us out of this," and *Flashman* was the result.

IDLER: You see, you are an Idler! Every Idler has to say to themselves at some point, "right, I'm going to go for it now and try and do the thing that I've always wanted to do."

GMF: Yes, that's true. I was glad that it happened, and I didn't expect it to happen, but I thought, "now's the time, now or never," you know?

IDLER: But the *Flashman* books have been such a huge success, did that surprise you?

GMF: Yes, totally.

IDLER: Because people are either completely obsessed with your books or they don't get them at all.

GMF: Well that is why it had such a difficult time getting published. As you say, you either think it's terrific or you don't. I've never been a publisher, thank God, and even when I was a features Editor I had no idea what was going to interest the public. I think that when publishers get something that they recognise they can have a good idea of how it will do. With *Flashman* they couldn't. It could either be a great success or it could fall flat on its face. And an awful lot of them said it would fall flat on its face until Herbert Jenkins took it. That was thanks to the efforts of George Greenfield the great agent.

IDLER: So he always believed in it?

GMF: That's right, I mean I was ready to give up but the other person who always believed in it was my wife who said, "No. Let's keep going. It's going to get published." And it did.

IDLER: These days trying to get a book published is like almost like making an advertising pitch, you have to bear in mind the sales potential from the start.

GMF: Is that right?

IDLER: I mean I don't think *Flashman* would get published today, which is a terrifying thought.

GMF: You're dead right. I was terribly lucky in the timing. Twenty years earlier and it wouldn't have got published. It was far too advanced in some ways, and now? Not a chance. Not in this politically correct day and age.

IDLER: I think one of the reasons it's so popular today is people's appetite for history. I was interested to read that one of your heroes was Robert Louis Stevenson, another great Idler I might add. He wrote a fantastic piece called *An Apology For Idlers* and he contributed to the *Idler* in the 1890s.

GMF: Did he really? I never knew that.

IDLER: It's a fantastic essay about how career-minded men can't bear the thought of society being indifferent to their achievements. So his argument was that by doing nothing you're actually being revolutionary.

GMF: I didn't know that, this would be in Jerome's time?

IDLER: That's right. Conan Doyle wrote for it as well back then.

GMF: Conan Doyle wrote for the *Idler*? That *is* interesting.

I read the other day of a dinner that has been all but forgotten, there is no record of it, where a publisher called Stoddart invited

FLASHMAN AND THE TIGER

Flashman, characteristically, is on the run...

'...At all costs I must avoid detection; there was only one thing for it—I was dressed like a soup-kitchen derelict, and in a twinkling I had poured the rest of my flask [of brandy] down my coat-front, sprawled down against a convenient grating, and was lying there wheezing like an intoxicated grampus, trying to look like a stupefied down-and-out who has crept in to doss for the night, when the footsteps turned out of the house and came towards me.

If they've any sense they'll just pass by, thinks I—well, don't you, when you see some ragged bummaree sleeping it off in the gutter? But no, curse their nosiness, they didn't. The footsteps stopped beside me, and I chanced a quick look at 'em through half-closed lids—a tall, slim

Oscar Wilde and Conan Doyle for dinner together. As a result of the meeting Doyle wrote *The Sign of Four* and Wilde wrote *The Picture of Dorian Gray.* And the only thing that Doyle remembered was that they discussed war and Wilde said, "It's getting to the stage where there won't be armies. Two chemists with test tubes will approach the frontline."

IDLER: No!

GMF: Isn't that amazing? But Conan Doyle and Oscar Wilde. That would've been interesting.

IDLER: That just reminded me of my favourite bit in *Flashman and the Tiger* where he's hiding in the street pretending to be a homeless drunk and Sherlock Holmes and Doctor Watson stumble across him. That's one of the greatest delights of your books, the meshing of historical fact with fictional characters.

GMF: Thank you.

IDLER: You must have had a real rush of pleasure when you had the idea to write that.

GMF: Oh yes, and of course Holmes gets it all wrong! [Laughs]

IDLER: ...and Flashman walks off fuming about being labelled a German! [both laughing] So will any more *Flashman* papers come to light?

GMF: Oh I don't know. Obviously they will never all be opened but I hope there will be one or two yet,

IDLER: You still have an appetite for writing them?

GMF: Oh yes, I mean I'm very glad when one is finished, you forget about it for a while but of course soon the bug takes over again.

IDLER: And then there was one Flashman film, *Royal Flash* with Malcolm McDowell. It's

cove in a long coat, bare-headed and balding, and a big, hulking chap with a bulldog moustache and hard hat. They looked like a poet and a bailiff.
"What's this?" says the bailiff, stooping over me.
"A tramp," says the poet. "One of the flotsam, escaping his misery in a few hours of drunken slumber."
"Think he's all right?" says the bailiff, rot him, and blow me if he wasn't fumbling for my pulse.
"Going at full gallop," says he, and blast his infernal impudence, he put a hand on my brow. "My goodness, but he's feverish. D'you think we should get help for him?"
"You'll get no thanks beyond a flood of curses if you do," says the poet carelessly. "Really, doctor, even without close examination my nose can tell me more than your fingers. The fellow is hopelessly under the influence of drink—and rather inferior drink, at that, I fancy," says he, stooping and sniffing at the fumes which were rising from my sodden breast. "Yes, American bourbon, unless I am mistaken. The odour is quite distinctive—you may have remarked that to the trained senses, each spirit has its own peculiar characteristics; I believe I have in the past drawn your attention to the marked difference between the rich, sugary aroma of rum, and the more delicate sweet smell of gin," says this amazing lunatic. "But what now?"
The bailiff, having taken his confounded liberties with my wrist and brow, was pausing in the act of trying to lift one of my eyelids, and his next words filled me with panic.
"Good Lord!" he exclaimed. "I believe I know this chap—but no, it can't be, surely! Only he's

incredibly hard to get hold of, were you happy with it?

GMF: It was all right, people vary, I didn't like it at the time but I've grown to have an affection for it. It's very interesting though, the bit parts, David Jason has one line in it. Bob Hoskins has a lovely little cameo, beautifully done. It was fun. I mean I thought there was too much send-up, too much slapstick. But as an adventure story I think it was told in an amusing way. It was looked at as a comedy.

IDLER: Do you think there will ever be any other *Flashman* films?

GMF: I doubt it. I think the time has gone really. David Niven told me he was desperate to play Flashman but as he said himself, he was too old.

IDLER: There was one final thing I wanted to ask you, who did the fantastic original Flashman covers?

GMF: Arthur Barbosa. A wonderful man, he was an interior decorator by trade. Richard Burton and Elizabeth Taylor had a yacht and that was one of his great jobs, to decorate it. He was a great mate of Rex Harrison, they went to art school together. But you see that [pointing at the cover picture of Flashman] is Arthur. He modelled Flashman on himself. I wasn't terribly pleased [laughing], but he did. And I have a photograph somewhere of *Flashman at the Charge* and the cover had Flashman with a sabre and a cossack's hat on and it was Arthur, with a poker in his hand and a tea cosy on his head! [laughing] But he was a very fine man and a very stylish artist. There's never been anyone quite like him.

uncommonly like that old general… oh, what's-his name? You know, made such a hash of the Khartoum business, with Gordon… yes, and years ago he won a great name in Russia, and the Mutiny—V.C. and knighthood—it's on the tip of my tongue—"

"My dear fellow," says the high-pitched poet, "I can't imagine who your general may be—it can hardly be Lord Roberts, I fancy—but it seems likely that he would chose to sleep in his home or his club, rather than in an alley. Besides," he went on wearily, stooping a little closer—and damned unnerving it was, to feel those two faces peering at me through the gloom, while I tried to sham insensible – "besides, this is a nautical, not a military man; he's not English, but either American or German—probably the latter, since he has certainly studied at a second-rate German university, but undoubtedly he has been in American quite lately. He is known to the police, is currently working as a ship's steward…for I observe that he has declined even from his modest beginnings—and will, unless I am greatly mistaken, be in Hamburg by the beginning of next week—provided he wakes up in time. More than that," says the know-all ignoramus…

"Well," says the other doubtfully, "I'm sure you're right, but he looks extremely like old what's-his-name. But how on earth can you tell so much about him from so brief a scrutiny?'

"You have not forgotten my methods since we last met, surely?" says the conceited ass, who I began to suspect was some kind of maniac…."

Flashman and the Tiger, *Harper Collins, £6.99*

EASY SOUNDS:

FIRE IN THE BLOOD

Karen Hooper meets Alabama 3's Larry Love. Photography by Gregor Smith

Alabama 3's lead singer Rob Spragg—also known as Larry Love—is looking every bit the outlaw frontman. He's wearing a white Stetson and customary shades as he holds court at Jamm, a new club in south London at an after show party and launch of Alabama 3's new album, Outlaw. Here, in the words of their ballad, "Adrenaline", "everyone's on the guest list to heaven".

Alabama 3's carnivalesque celebration of the outsider is matched by their deep-rooted sense of justice. Recently they've been supporting MOJO, the Miscarriages of Justice Organisation. They played a gig at Shepherds Bush Empire to launch MOJO's campaign to raise £500,000 to set up what they call a Retreat for the Innocent. MOJO works to free and support men and women who have been wrongfully imprisoned. MOJO is fronted by "Birmingham Six" Paddy Hill, who was denied his liberty for 17 years and John McManus, a sharp-tongued former trade unionist. At Shepherds Bush McManus took to the stage in a MOJO t-shirt, with the Daniel Defoe quote: "I hear much of people's calling out to punish the guilty, but few are concerned to clear the innocent."

The Retreat, which MOJO hopes to set up within two years, will act as a "depressurizing chamber"; a safe environment to deal with post-traumatic stress disorder and to try and halt the depression and drug abuse that sets in about nine months after a prisoner attains "freedom".

"The Alabamas have been invaluable and we wouldn't have got as far as we are now without them," says McManus of the band's support. The track "The Thrills Have Gone", on Alabama's second album, *La Peste*, is dedicated to Pady Hill.

Says Love of Hill: "He's got these piercing eyes and when those eyes look at you, they can be intimidating, but you see a very wise and powerful man who's worked tirelessly for justice."

MOJO's ethos fits comfortably with Alabama 3's preoccupations. Their website takes as its theme "the ever pervasive concept of penal rehabilitation" and goes on to say: "We are all in prison. By 2010, 9.46 per cent of the population will be related to someone suffering the perils of incarceration."

"We've come full circle. *Exile on Coldharbour Lane* was the blueprint. We started *Outlaw* with the drums and let it grow organically. We describe the music as techno, house beats fused with blues and western sensibility, acid house country."

The band started when Love met co-frontman Jake Black, aka The Very Reverend D. Wayne Love, during the rave years. It was a match made in heaven. Love is the son of a Mormon preacher from the valleys of

TOP: ZOE DEVLIN. BOTTOM: NICK REYNOLDS, LARRY LOVE, JAKE BLACK

South Wales and Black was brought up by trade union Marxists in Glasgow.

Most people will be familiar with their music from *The Sopranos*, whose theme music is the Alabama's song "Woke Up This Morning". The track is based on the case of Sarah Thornton who stabbed her abusive husband and Love transposed the story to a US trailer park.

"I didn't intend for people to take the lyrics literally," says Love. "As artists we respond to the chaos around us. Grime music responds to the

WHAT'S MY NAME? JOHNNY CASH!

abandoned inner cities, crack and the lack of an adequate detox plan; it's in context.

"If you listen to the blues and country, Leadbelly, Muddy Waters, Johnny Cash, it's part of prison culture… it pays homage to the downtrodden; that's inspired me."

A meeting with Bruce Reynolds, mastermind of the Great Train Robbery, inspired the latest album. Love liked Reynolds' fascination with the search for the lost city of El Dorado. Reynolds appears on the album track "Bruce Richard Reynolds", based on an East End folk song.

The song "How Can I Protect You?", samples from "Lay Lady Lay" and is dedicated to Love's five-year-old daughter Nansi. Love is pleased that Nansi is mixing with children from diverse cultures at her nursery in south London. She also accompanies her dad on his cultural recces. "I took her to the Caravaggio exhibition and left her drawing one of the milder paintings, while I went off to look at the violent decapitated heads stuff."

Love is inspired by gutsy women. "Up Above My Head" takes its cue from Sister Rosetta Tharpe, a radical female guitarist from an early Bo Diddley line-up. "Honey in The Rock" welcomes a promising newcomer in Zoe Devlin.

"Let It Slide" opens to a haunting version of the Stones' "Gimme Shelter".

"It's about this mad drug-fuelled drive I took across Dublin; about the smack epidemic, Es and Jack Daniels, fuckin' scary… driving over roundabouts, as the French say, the 'Little Death of orgasm'."

Love is adamant that "real artists steal", rather than sample, and *Outlaw* is a game in recognising great moments across music genres. The single "Hello… I'm Johnny Cash", steals the country king's best lines.

"It's about a crisis in masculine identity, paying homage to that working class thing in Wales of the guy who brings his pay home to his missus, but at night he does his quiff and can still go out and be Johnny Cash."

Love's early years in South Wales are clearly mapped onto his stage persona. "The Mormon hymnbook taught me a lot about American gospel music, which is the foundation of Alabama 3's unique country and western techno soul," he says. The Mormons colonized South Wales during the Industrial Revolution, "put in context, there's 891 pubs and 892 chapels. But they also had a well-developed welfare system and looked after the poorest."

School liberated him from his "religious cul-de-sac". His English and art teachers inspired him. The alternative was "two years on a Mormon mission knocking on doors."

"I emphasized with Keats and his enjoyment of taking black pepper on his tongue and then necking down his favourite claret to enhance the burn... 'With beaded bubbles, winking at the brim'... That idea of loads of pain and a bit of pleasure in 'Ode to a Nightingale', has fuelled my artistic endeavour ever since. When I encountered Lou Reed and the Velvet Underground, there was a sense of a similar literary awakening. 'Waiting for the Man' is classic poetry."

Love's parents tried to censor his records, but didn't manage the books: "they couldn't hear me reading." By 15, he'd discovered Burroughs' *Naked Lunch* and "all about Molly Bloom's period pains in Joyce's *Ulysses*'. In an attempt to redeem him, the Mormon bishop let his first band, Wynsloyn Jones and the Gravediggers, rehearse in the local chapel, "but we were fermenting a rebellion from within".

Love read law at Aberyswyth University. "I did my dissertation on D.H. Lawrence and the obscenity trials and called it 'Dirty Bertie And His Friends Go To Court'." He refused a place at Oxford.

"I was always conscious of class polarity given the miners' struggle and am the only person in my family to go to university". At one university interview, he says, "all they saw was this scummy Welsh kid from a two-bedroomed council flat in a pair of horrible brown nylon trousers." When they asked why he wanted to study law he said:

"I'M INSPIRED BY THE POLITICAL AWAKENING OF YOUNG PEOPLE INVOLVED IN A GLOBAL STRUGGLE"

"Because I enjoy watching Crown Court. Obviously they told me to fuck off.

"After university I moved to London and worked in hostels for the homeless... My politics were quite localised when I was younger, like the miners' strike, but I'm inspired by the political awakening of young people involved in a more globalised struggle."

Love has taken strength from the alienating experience of being the "kid who took a kicking in the playground for being Mormon" and the split identity of being Welsh. His irreverence and resistance towards all social programming extends to those in the music industry who wave their flags. Love's an optimist on a covert operation: "Think of it as the shape shifting Welsh armies who covered themselves in blue wode and went into battle in the half light as the sun was going down and terrorized the Romans."

www.alabama3.co.uk

EASY SOUNDS:

QUINTRON & MISS PUSSYCAT

Sarah Janes meets the New Orleans duo

Quintron and Miss Pussycat are a two-piece, swamp tech, showbiz extravaganza from New Orleans. Quintron is an organist and inventor. In concerts he energetically plays a home made Hammond/Rhodes synthesizer-keyboard-motorcar hybrid (with flashing headlights and Louisiana plates) whilst simultaneously working his own patented invention—The Drum Buddy™ (an oscillating, light-activated analogue drum machine synthesizer). High energy, electric, sweat-drenched, unpredictable and occasionally violent, Quintron's one-man musical mutant chaos is always interesting and exciting with showers of sparkling rhinestones, sexy outfits, bright colours, addictive beats and sing-a-long sound bites.

Miss Pussycat is a world-famous puppeteer whose legendary puppet band Flossie and The Unicorns were a favourite of John Peel and even came to England to do a session for his Radio 1 show. Every Quintron and Miss Pussycat concert begins with Miss Pussycat's highly entertaining puppet show featuring her instantly recognisable, loveably colourful characters and "humanettes". Miss Pussycat is also a talented dress-maker, a supremely creative make'n'doer and adds something extra glamorous and special, the like of which has never seen in a nightclub no place no how nowhere. Miss Pussycat sings back up and plays maracas, too.

Brighton LOVED Quintron and Miss Pussycat and after the show they had a small but devout Brighton following who still talk about their performance a year and four months later! After the show we went back to my friend Gabriel's house and stayed up very late drinking pints of red wine and cementing our friendship. We invented new animals, we phoned up a certain record label and left drunken death threats on their answerphone, we listened to lots of music, we drew pictures, we laughed and laughed and laughed. I laughed so much that when I woke up the following morning my whole body ached and my face had creases in from smiling so hard. It was a fantastic night. To celebrate, we had a cream tea for breakfast and Quintron and Miss Pussycat were immediately won over by the spoon-bending qualities of clotted cream. Then they were off to catch a ferry and we vowed to meet again, if not in Merrie Olde England, then in New Orleans.

A mere matter of months later, Quintron and Miss Pussycat were invited to play Southern Comfort's Fat Tuesday tent at the Big Chill festival and so they duly got me a ticket. The tent was done up Mardi Gras style and everyone got feather masks and boas during Q and P's performance

SWAMP-TECH SHOWBIZ EXTRAVAGANZA FROM NEW ORLEANS

which was characteristically brilliant and had everyone dancing and singing. The following day we decided to take the day off and explore a bit of the local countryside, indulging in cream teas, Pimms, car boot sales and gymkhanas. It was glorious sunshine and excellent fun and the next couple of days rolled along much the same.

Next came my turn to go over to New Orleans, and no time could be better than Mardi Gras. I booked three weeks away and as the day of my flight drew nearer I became increasingly excited about seeing my dear pals again. On the day I flew out I received an email from Quintron

JONATHON TRAVIESA

saying "by the time you read this you will have been whisked off into the night by a pink limousine". I chuckled to myself as I checked in.

When I got to New Orleans airport there was no sign of Quintron or Miss Pussycat. I was starting to think that something had happened and after 45 minutes of pondering, stood in a taxi queue outside. At precisely that moment, the airport lights glinted off a long pink bonnet and a pink limousine glided alongside the curb. Quintron had been going round the block for an hour. He was dressed as a chauffeur and it was the perfect airport pick-up.

Quintron and Miss Pussycat live just outside the French Quarter in an amazing double-shotgun mansion on St. Claude Avenue. They have a secret marine-themed nightclub in their basement called the Spellcaster Lodge where Peaches, Jon Spencer and Andre Williams have played among many others. They have a scary cat called Sparky and a not-as-frisky-as-he-used-to-be ferret called Tiger that lives in a ferret-sized pink castle. For three weeks I was a resident at the Spellcaster Lodge. Q and P provided me with my very own bicycle and I went riding every day through beautiful New Orleans. There were lots of parties and lots of shows. Their annual Maritime Ball was held at the Spellcaster and Q and P did a big show at one of New Orleans best venues, One Eyed Jacks (I did the lighting) it was a particularly good show that night. The performance started off with a gay mechanic dance routine (lots of baby oil and short shorts) and at the end Miss P passed out behind one of the monitors and had to be carried back to the van. All in all a great evening!

The next day was Mardi Gras and it was the most surreal, beautiful and balmy day, wandering around the French Quarter. Everyone was lolling around in fancy dress, most people having been awake 48 hours and looking like glamorous zombies. The mist was rolling in off the Mississippi. Glittering beads and streamers draped over wrought iron balconies. Marching bands stopping to play under big concrete highways, stir your very spinal chord and potent cocktails dizzy your blood.

Back home there was a blizzard in Blighty. Quintron and Miss Pussycat and I had discussed me organizing a UK tour at some point in the future and I got stuck into plans straight away, very excited about bringing Q and P back to the UK. The Mars Volta invited them to play All Tomorrow's Parties "Nightmare Before Christmas" event in Camber Sands and very quickly dozens of other requests came in.

Over summertime, Quintron and Miss Pussycat were touring mainland Europe and I went to meet them for my birthday in Amsterdam. I had a birthday space cake and we partied in a strange Latino cab driver bar (with porn on a big screen) till 4am, a whitey was pulled and we went our separate ways till now, when I am going out to New Orleans again.

Quintron and Miss Pussycat's forthcoming release 'Swamp Tech' (a double-disc set featuring Miss Pussycat's puppet movie 'Electric Swamp') is out on Transsolar Records (in Berlin, Tigerbeat6 in the US) on October 17th. Quintron and Miss Pussycat's 15 date December UK Tour 'Swamp Tech' will include All Tomorrow's Parties, 2-4th of December. For more details go to: www.quintronandmisspussycat.com

IDLE PURSUITS:

PLAYING THE LONG GAME

Ben Moor revels in the crack of leather on willow. Illustration by Anthony Haythornthwaite

My school was just past the county ground of Kent and I spent the summers of the mid-1980s dropping in after school (entry was free after tea for county games) watching a fairly decent county side do fairly well in fairly good weather. My girlfriend was at the equivalent girls school, and we'd meet in the Frank Woolley Stand, read each other our History essays, kiss, admire the lime tree in the middle of the field (which has since fallen) and generally live in what was then the acceptable present but what I now realise to be a perfect past. We could have been doing homework or after school jobs, but lazing what was were spending our time on and the cricket was the perfect venue.

There are other crickety moments of that time—seeing the 1985 Australians jogging around Canterbury, watching Viv Richards wallop sixes there for Somerset—and in fact every time I take one from the old library of memory, I smile. Watching cricket has so much going for it for the professional idler and we should thank the English Gods we weren't born in a country where the main sports involve doing things very quickly or shouting.

Explain to an American how a day of test cricket works and that play stops for lunch and tea and enjoy their baffled faces. But surely a sport whose breaks are defined not precisely by the passage of time but by the need to eat knows its priorities. Even the mid-session break called "drinks" (which I think should be termed "coffee" in the morning session and "cocktails" in the later afternoon) works as good as anything in suggesting the ultimate easiness of the game. Not that it's easy to play, just that it takes thing easily.

At least Test cricket does. In 1912 the craze was to play timeless tests where the game would last as long as it took. I also miss the rest days they used to schedule in, in case the pace of the game was increasing dangerously from a stroll to meander.

For One Day Cricket is for people whose idea of fishing involves a barrel and a shotgun. It's like using crack for cake decorating. It might give you a thrill, but it spoils something that is sweet enough. But things have got worse. There is now the new frenzied abomination which is Twenty20 cricket where the aim is to speed up the game in order to appeal to our ADHD afflicted youth. They have destroyed the pavillion and put the batting side

on a bench on the boundary and batsmen have to run to the wicket or they are called out before facing a ball. For the sake of all that is holy, why? Yes, modern life is fast and busy and full of arbitrary punishments, but cricket has always been filled with beautiful metaphors of an earlier age, such as asking politely for decisions and being caught out by a silly point.

There is the glorious possibility that on any given ball exactly nothing will happen. Can there be any idler moment than when a batsman leaves a full length ball outside his off stump, it goes through to the keeper, the scorer marks it as a dot, a black hole of nothingness on the card, the crowd mumbles and has another look at the crossword, the batter dabs at the pitch, the sun shines, the grass grows, the ball is gently returned to the bowler like a soft laugh and the whole process can begin again. Now some might find that scenario deathly dull, but they don't see the poetry in stillness.

For those that do, and those who appreciate the imposition of stillness in the modern world, cricket can prompt enormous amounts of idleness. A day at a test match is a day spent drinking and watching events happening a hundred yards away or more; look away briefly and you might miss the crucial moment. But still they come, especially on the final day when prices are cheaper. The thousands who turned up with me at Lords on the fifth day of the New Zealand test match last year weren't there because they had nothing more important to do—I imagine a lot of them had actual jobs that involved them having to do actual work—but because this was better than that. In September 2000 I tried in vain to get into The Oval to watch the last day of that Test summer. But it was full with slackers who had got there first to witness our first series victory over the West Indies in a thousand years. Luckily I spotted a friend in a window that had a great view of the ground and he let me up to watch the climax there. Another happy moment provided by the greatest game in the world.

But my experience is not entirely as a watcher.

THERE IS THE GLORIOUS POSSIBILITY THAT EXACTLY NOTHING WILL HAPPEN

As a student at one of the country's older univeristies, I was a member of a cricket team called the Utopers. We had a distinctly leisurely approach to the game.

We'd always try to field first, partly out of politeness, but mainly so we could take our pints of warm summer beer out to the park and drink while we fielded. Then when the opponents had set their total we'd drink more in the pavilion while waiting for our turn to bat, then we'd bat a bit, and after we were out we'd drink more in the pavilion. Some memories provoke such heaven that no other sport can really compare. I was a rugby player too at college—not a bad one either—but those cricket matches just have that glow around them in my mind. I think my top score was sixteen or something, I took maybe a couple of jammy wickets and probably dropped more catches than I held on to, but when it came to enjoying those game afternoons I was a champion.

A champion at combining the greatest game in the world—cricket—and the greatest joy of life—idling.

GARDENING:

PERMACULTURE

Graham Burnett on doing it yourself

An episode of the Australian TV series *Global Gardener* features Bill Mollison demonstrating the making of his permaculture garden. Planting through sheet mulches of newspaper and straw, he claims to have created a landscape able to satisfy all of his needs for food, wood, medicine and fibres in less than thirty working days over a three-year period. "And this is where the designer turns into the recliner," he winks.

Permaculture is a concept that is beautifully simple, yet can be notoriously difficult to explain. But "creating abundant and sustainable human habitats by following nature's patterns" is a useful sound-bite summary.

Permaculture isn't about having to get your head around untold facts, figures, Latin names and complicated techniques. Advocated instead is contemplative observation of natural systems in order to see universal patterns and principles at work. These are then applied to meeting our own needs using minimum effort for maximum effect. For example, if we are to feed ourselves sustainably we clearly need to be moving away from industrialized agriculture and more towards a gardening philosophy—less high chemical input prairie farming of monocultures and more market and home gardens; places for creating edible landscapes, community growing projects and forest gardens.

Not many of us would be able to grow *all* of the food we need to live, but most of could make a significant contribution to our own diets. I haven't had to buy onions or garlic for years, and soft fruits practically come out of our earholes in the summer, as do broad and runner beans, tomatoes and courgettes. Homegrown potatoes are available from summer to winter solstice, and plenty of other crops come and go throughout the productive season. It's probably true to say that every family meal throughout the year will include at least one thing that is from our garden or allotment, even if it's just a handful of winter chard. Growing your own not only guarantees a supply of fresh, locally grown produce, but has many other benefits—exercise and stress relief (I particularly like Mollison's description of gardening as a "gentle form of Tai Chi"), a reconnection with the soil or an excuse to simply lean on the spade and philosophise the afternoon away.

Permaculture is a personal thing, but there are a few ground rules to follow:

- Work with nature, not against it. For example, using mulches rather than digging will encourage worms to cultivate the soil and keep it moist, and planting flowers like poached egg plants and marigolds, or making a pond will attract pest controlling ladybirds and frogs.
- Create diversity. Grow as wide and mixed a variety of fruits, nuts and vegetables as possible (a polyculture), not just row upon row of one thing. Monocultures aren't just boring, they are a disaster waiting to happen—remember the Irish Potato Famine of 1845.

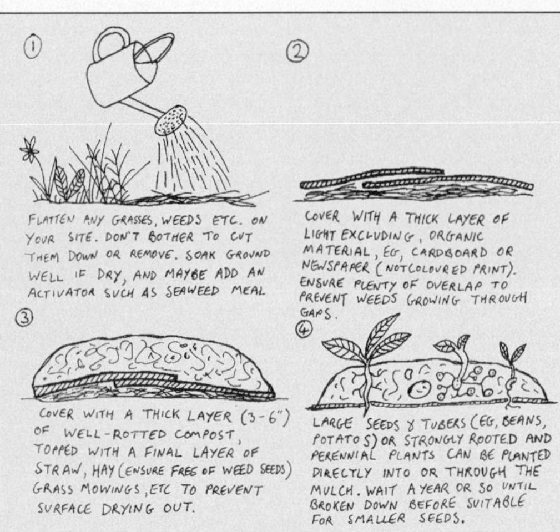

WE CARE A LOT

- Close the broken cycles. Compost your kitchen waste, don't put it in landfill pits—or better still, install a compost toilet to stop your own "wastes" from being flushed out to sea...
- See solutions instead of problems. Those nettles between your cropping areas aren't weeds they are a resource. You can eat them in soup or make them into beer, use them to create rope, dyes and fertiliser plus they are medicinal and provide a habitat for wildlife.
- Put things in the right place. There's not a lot of point in planting "Cut 'n' Come Again" lettuces on your allotment two miles away from your house. When you are knocking up a salad for tea, human nature and the law of minimum effort dictates that you will pop round to the greengrocers and buy a lettuce whilst your crop sits and runs to seed. It makes more sense to put those elements that require frequent picking or attention—salad plants, herbs, strawberries, seedlings in trays—close to the back door where that best of all fertilisers, "the gardener's shadow", most often falls.

What I like about permaculture is that it asks us to start from where we are now; "at the end of your nose," as Bill Mollison says. You don't have to wait until "After The Revolution" to sprout a jar of beans on your kitchen shelf. Starting an organic allotment or planting an apple tree are positive steps towards creating healthy self-reliant communities. At its essence, permaculture is about that old "green truism", "Think Globally But Act Locally". For cliché or not, that is where the future lies if we are to have one.

Graham is the writer and illustrator of 'Permaculture a Beginners Guide' and runs permaculture courses at Dial House (also home of Camp Idle). For more information see www.spiralseed.co.uk

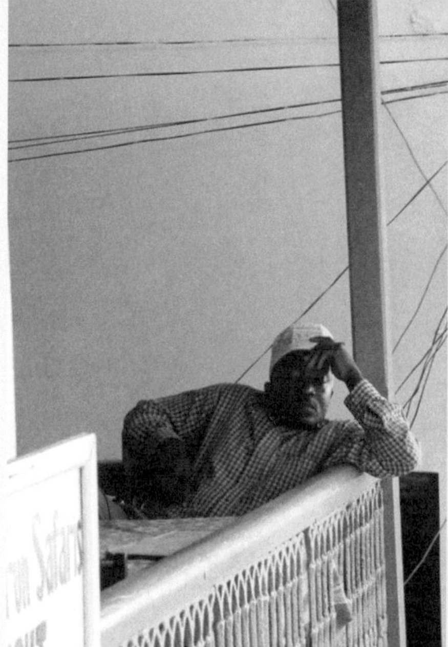

TOP: CHRISTMAS ARRIVES, BOTTOM LEFT: TAKING IT EASY, BOTTOM RIGHT: PEMBA

TRAVEL:

TANZANIA

Clare Dowdy finds laid back locals and frenetic tourists. Pics by Giles Godwin

Tanzanians are masters of the art of appearing relaxed. This is particularly the case when it comes to earning a living. However, this should not be read as an African version of the "mañana" ethic of Latin America.

The country, on the east coast of Africa, rubs shoulders with Kenya, Uganda, Rwanda, Democratic Republic of Congo, Burundi, Zambia, Malawi, and Mozambique. It is one of the poorest countries in the world—with half the thirty-three million people living below the poverty line. Unemployment is high, so any semblance of slacking has more to do with the lack of job opportunities than the actual work ethic or mindset.

For those with jobs, the commute is likely to involve a cycle ride. This will appear a leisurely affair, with men pedalling their Chinese Phoenixes or Indian-made Raleights [sic] at little more than walking pace. However, these hefty bikes have no gears and the roads mostly comprise dust and pot holes, so speed is not really an option.

The few decent roads are likely to be constructed by the Chinese, who are big investors in Tanzania and like to have the infrastructure to export their produce.

This is an egalitarian country, where the women—even on Tanzania's Muslim island of Zanzibar—are very much part of the workplace. For many Zanzibaris, the workplace is the Indian Ocean. For much of the day, these ladies—sometimes accompanied by their offspring—stroll through the shallows in long dresses. However, rather than taking their daily constitutional, they are harvesting seaweed. And as the tide turns, they go back to their village to lay out the seaweed in front of their house. The next part of the job involves literally watching seaweed dry. From there, it is taken to a Philippino-owned factory for processing.

This drying process is not dissimilar to that of the country's most famous produce, cloves. The fifty mile-long island of Pemba, just off Zanzibar, is where most of the clove action happens. Again, cloves are picked in their pale pink and soft state, and laid out—this time in elaborate patterns—to dry. The issue of cloves is enough to make the blood of the most tranquil Tanzanians boil, for the Government is accused of price fixing. In fact the only real sign of law enforcement is the roadblocks on Pemba, which are intended to detect clove smuggling.

One of the few occasions when tempers became frayed during my visit to this part of Africa was during a village dance. A fêted Taraab band from Zanzibar Town was doing an al fresco gig. For this special occasion, the girls and young ladies of the village of Jambiani had dressed appropriately, and in their long, formal dresses and strappy sandals, none would have looked out of place as brides

TOP: STONETOWN DOES RETAIL, BOTTOM: RE-CYCLING TANZANIAN STYLE maids. The men, of course, were in T-shirts and jeans. The music, a sort of African, Indian and Arabic *mélange*, induced much good-humoured swaying. All was going smoothly until a scuffle broke out between a young couple, resulting in fisticuffs and her dress coming away in his hands. The music didn't miss a beat and the incident was soon forgotten.

The appearance of laziness continues into the night, when it is not unusual to see people actually asleep on the job. Pemba's main metropolis, Chake Chake (pronounced Chucky Chucky), holds a night food market along the pavements—if there were any—of the high street. Anyone who has delighted in the frenzied hassling and hawking of Zanzibar Town's tourist-heavy-native-light night market will find the Chake Chake experience wholly underwhelming. Here, the stalls are lit by single candles and the stall holders are found stretched out behind their tasty offerings (doughnuts of the sweet and savoury varieties) often having to be woken up by their hungry clientele.

Chake Chake is also home to the Pemba Press Club, which supports the island's 70 reporters. In this hot, dark room comprising a few computers, a couple of phones, a fan and a stereo displayed with its polystyrene packaging still in place, there is a real campaigning spirit. The main issues for Pemba's 300 000 people are education and health. However, any sense of urgency is thwarted by the lack of Internet access. This means that stories have make their laborious progress to newspapers in the Tanzanian city of Dar Es Salaam by fax.

The average Tanzanian village is full of chatty people to whom the greeting of "Hello, how are you, welcome"—which in Swahili goes "Jambo, harbari, karibu"—trips off the tongue with almost North American regularity. The atmosphere is convivial, though the architecture can let the place down. It's not unusual to see half built houses lining the streets, which give the environs a sense of abandonment. A falling out with the builder, perhaps? Cowboy workmanship? More likely, as we were informed by local man Captain Zappo, funds run out before the house can be finished.

The pace of life may be slow, but it is also arduous for most Tanzanians. Though that doesn't mean they are missing out on all that modern life can offer. The Amani Nature Reserve, a few hours north of the mainland city of Dar Es Salaam is pretty remote by anyone's standards. Most villages in the reserve are unconnected by roads. However, they are connected by telecommunications. The locals make a beeline for a certain hilltop in the forest, for they know that's the best reception to check their mobile phone messages. The "call to prayer" ring tone is particularly popular in these parts.

The people who are the most conspicuously industrious are the swarms of do-gooding Westerners who have invaded the place. It is par for the course to run into all manner of aid workers, from people transmitting lessons to children on a special radio station to malaria researchers, from Oxfam officials to translators of the bible into Swahili. When they get chatting, they serve several useful purposes to the uninitiated. They shed a different light on the place, they make a pleasant change from safari and diving tourists (both total bores in their own way, going on about what wildlife they got relatively close to that day), and they are having to work while holidaymakers can legitimately put their feet up.

FILM:

THE WALL STREET SCUFFLE

Paul Hamilton on money in the movies

It was in the 1987 flick *Wall Street* where Oliver Stone's creation Gordon Gekko, the billionaire markets player and asset-stripper made reptilian flesh by Michael Douglas, personified the new greedbreed of the Reagan/Thatcher era. However, beyond its smattering of Gekkoid aphorisms—"Money never sleeps," "Greed is good, greed is right, greed works," "If you need a friend, get a dog," "Lunch is for wimps", adopted by the yuppies as new commandments for their age-old faith—*Wall Street* is a loathsome, rancid work of artistic and moral cowardice. Far from painting Gekko as the dark heart of mercantilism, he is rendered heroic by his macchiavellian misdeeds; his self-serving betrayals and backstabbings are imbued with a cavalier nobility by stockbroker's son Stone. This is regretful as it is nigh unavoidable in a country whose currency is stamped "In God We Trust"—despite the Bible's axiom of money being the root of all evil.

America loves its heroes and anti-heroes, the bigger the better. Whereas the British of yore would engage in a Sherlock Holmes unraveller or a Biggles airborne Bosche-bash, Americans would settle for no less than Superman. Gekko is a cartoon, taken from life and then ludicrously lubricated into an almost surreal form. Michael Douglas beams warm smiles but the eyes are cold as death. He is what one expects to greet you after you've been transported across the River Styx. He is as slippery as his gel-drowned hair. The Wall Street money marketeers can easily assuage feelings of liability and responsibility as they hold the livelihoods of people, communities, countries in their sweaty palms by pretending it's all a game, that they're just playing with numbers. Gekko's soul is immune from venality. Money is his meat and blood is his drink. Douglas' performance is so magnetic, he overpowers and overthrows the film. One needs to see his shambling, lost, dope-head English professor in *Wonder Boys*—he's *The Big Lebowski*'s Dude with mortar board and cape—to gauge the range and excellence of his acting. But whereas in *Wonder Boys* he has an exotic centre, a romantic ideal in his heart, in *Wall Street* he has none. Gekko has no heart. When Oliver Stone places Gekko on the beach in The Hamptons, rhapsodising the beauty of the tides, or when he dandles his son on his lap—Stone maybe making a comparison with Gestapo officers who are cold-blooded in their work yet warm, attentive and loving with their families at home—it is resoundingly bogus.

Wall Street's plot concerns Bud Fox (Charlie Sheen), an ambitious stockbroker, conflicting with his socialist dad (played by his real father, Martin Sheen) who is a union bigwig for an airline company that his son ends up running when Gekko, the

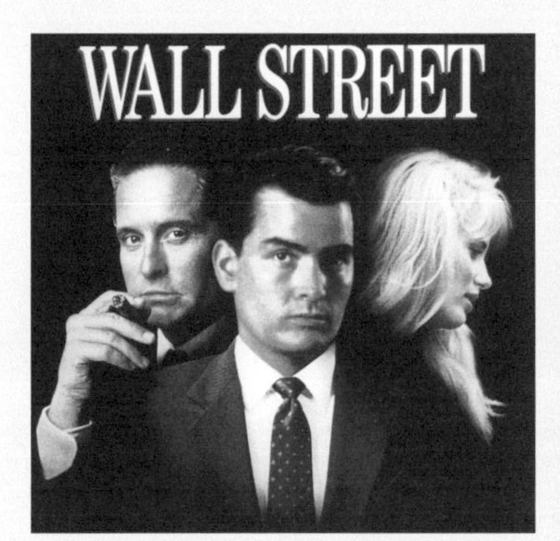

OLIVER STONE'S *WALL STREET*

brilliant lightbulb to Fox's moth, takes it over. Yes, it really is as dumb and shallow as it seems. And it is delivered in some of the worst soapbox dialogue ever written, more lumpen and stiff than Dalek shit. Each time Martin Sheen starts speechifying, one expects a huge flashing "AUTHOR'S MESSAGE!" sign to be plastered across the screen. Similarly, Hal Holbrook, playing one of the old boys in Bud Fox's office, is given "DEEP METAPHORS!" to intone gravely every time he appears onscreen to drape a friendly arm along Bud's young shoulders.

The film is no better than a middling-quality episode of *Dallas*, and only Douglas dares to go to the perimeters of Larry Hagman's dollarbilious tycoon loon J.R. Ewing. *Dallas* (and the equally daft *Dynasty*) was the epitome of money madness. Rather than discuss something on the telephone, the Ewings would traverse the States in private jets just to burst into an enemy's office simply to tell them to go to Hell. Oliver Stone regrettably lacks the mental springs to make such imaginative leaps. He is a pedestrian, humourless, gung-ho liberal, and his work is stained with that hollow Hollywood brand of socialism—the kind that hates socialists. (He's a one-man Labour Party.)

Stone's inability to understand women is apparent in his calamitous miscasting of Darryl Hannah as the art dealer and apex of the love triangle with Gekko and Fox. Hannah is too new age lentil-bean nice to be a conniving, two-faced, avaricious bitch. Stone required a Jennifer Jason Leigh to carry that weight convincingly, although even she would have had her work cut out giving substance to the inane dialogue. (One man who could write deliriously well for women is Greatest Living Englishman George Melly who scripted the 1968 film *Smashing Time*. Rita Tushingham and Lynn Redgrave are a pair of plain Janes who venture south to Swinging London to seek their fortune. They do so when Redgrave becomes a pop star and fashion icon, but as her celebrity damages her friendship with Tushingham, she quits and they bugger off back Oop North. A sweet, silly, splendid film.)

Wall Street has its protagonists in their big red braces chasing money, clinching deals on their housebrick-sized mobile phones round the clock. It's obsessional and the obsessive is never satisfied. The rare moments of personal pleasure are detected in the predatory Gekko's flaring his nostrils when the scent of a kill fills the air. But what do the über-nouveau riche do with their zillions? Money can't buy love and neither can it purchase taste. Look at the ghastly but trendy artworks cluttering their garish homes—the terrible daubs of Julian Schnabels—that speak of nothing other than their assumed market worth. Gekko again (the only times that the dialogue bursts into life is when he speaks): "Money itself is neither lost nor made. It is simply transferred from one perception to another, like magic. This painting here? I bought it ten years ago for $60,000. I could sell it today for [$600,000]. The illusion has become real, and the more real it becomes the more desperate they want it. Capitalism at its finest!"

Despite its being made on a multi-million bucks budget, *Wall Street* suffers from a poverty of verbal and visual inspiration. Terry Gilliam's *Jabberwocky* (1977)—fuelled by the hallucinogenic lyricism of Lewis Carroll and the hellish visions of Heironymus Bosch—is the direct opposite, a sumptuous feast of aural and visual delights made for a pittance. Gilliam's scenic compositions also owe much to Pieter Bruegel and Caravaggio but are not mere slavish copies. Lacking the cash to build a medieval castle, strategically placed black drapes produce the effect of the vastness of King Olaf's cobwebbed and squalid palace. Fiscal strictures unleashes Gilliam's creativity: Compare the richnesses and boldness of the El Cheapo *Jabberwocky* to the bloated, joyless, vacuous two hour yawn of his later $40m flop *The Adventures Of Baron Munchausen*.

Jabberwocky was made during the mid-1970s, a time of capitalism in deep crisis (nationwide strikes, fuel shortages, inflation in Britain hitting double figures, and unemployment figures hitting the million mark for the first time in forty years) and, although set in the middle ages, it reflects and comments on the chaos and renting of the social fabric outside the film studio. Gilliam employs the standard *Monty Python* joke device of transferring 20th century archetypes to the pre-industrial era. Michael Palin is Dennis, a cooper's apprentice harbouring ambitions to be a stocktaker or accountant—a less caricatured version of his spectacularly dull Eric Olthwaite and Arthur Putey personas. He can't resist "trying to improve the business" or increasing productivity and efficiency, and each attempt is met with catastrophic results. Meanwhile, the land is being terrorised by a savage beast, the jabberwock—a metaphor for the twin monstrous threats of unemployment and starvation. The merchants are pleased by the menace—it keeps their fearful workers' heads down and accepting of miniscule pay and torturously long hours. The church, too, welcomes the Fear—it keeps the temples full and gives the populace something to pray about. As a drama, *Jabberwocky* is flawed—there are too many jokes and digressions (Gilliam is desperately pouring everything he can into these two hours as though this is his only chance to make a film; a charge he is guilty of in every film he makes.) The

TERRY GILLIAM'S *JABBERWOCKY*, STARRING MICHAEL PALIN

plot—what there is of it—is almost swamped to the point of incoherence, but at its heart *Jabberwocky* poetically captures a society in a state of hysterical panic. In the economic depression, Dennis' one possession, a rotten potato, becomes a valuable form of currency. Gilliam cameos as a forest-dwelling loon believing his meagre pit of stones is a diamond mine ("Money itself is neither lost nor made. It is simply transferred from one perception to another"). In the fortified, dilapidated city-cum-asylum, costermongers are scarce. Instead, raucous rag-wrapped human scarecrows roam the market square hawking freshly killed rats for the dinner table—an ominous preview of the rat plague of 1978 following strikes by dustmen and undertakers. Dennis encounters legendary barrel maker Wat Dabney (Jerold Wells) who, despite his celebrity as inventor of the inverted firkin, can't get a job. In order to make some

money to buy some yummy rats Dabney has hacked off his right foot for improved begging potential ("a golden business opportunity," he merrily informs Dennis).

Gilliam is a rarity amongst modern film directors in creating amusing roles for women. (Usually in film comedies the pretty blond love interest stands aside while the men do their crazy stuff; Christine Taylor in *Zoolander*, for instance.) Here he casts Deborah Fallender, an unselfconscious Uma

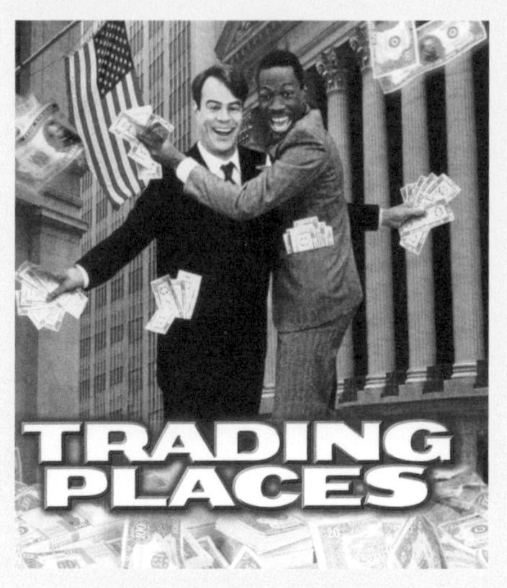

JOHN LANDIS'S *TRADING PLACES*

Thurman, as a potty princess, her silly head full of fairy tale derring-do and soppy Barbara Cartland romance. Gilliam also displays a novel touch of reverse sexism: Dennis slays the beast and is rewarded with the king's daughter's hand in marriage—but he still hankers for the affections of sluttish slobby uncaring Griselda Fishfinger (Annette Badlands).

On the *Jabberwocky* DVD commentary track, Terry Gilliam states that this was an anti-Hollywood film and his attack came in the form of celebrating what Hollywood perceives as ugliness—ancient, withered, wrinkled, saggy people besmirched in dirt and excreta (Palin is urinated upon twice), their teeth resembling vandalised tombstones or lumps of hard cheese. King Olaf's personal guards are obese wobblechops barely contained in their frayed, steaming chainmail. No suntans here. Everyone bears the same sickly pale yellow complexion as Dennis' prized spud. There is a profound enchantment in the rich and abundantly diverse array of faces here—Max Wall, John Le Mesurier, Warren Mitchell, Annette Badlands and Uncle Ken Colley and all. Gilliam recognises a beautiful harmony of humanity. Against this, the luminous perfect gnashers and the perfect pampered sun-kissed skin of *Wall Street*'s stars are disturbingly fascistic in their bland uniformity. Even the beggars, glimpsed from Gekko's limo, seem to be dressed by Armani (or, at least, Armani and Navy). I can't even recall a significant black character mixing with *Wall Street*'s parade of Aryan perfection, although I did notice Eddie Murphy in *Trading Places*, the 1983 *Wall St.*-based comedy. But then, who didn't?

Trading Places has an intriguing premise: If an uneducated, socially-disadvantaged black beggar swapped places with a university-graduated upper class white stockbroker, would the black man adapt to his new luxurious surroundings and high-powered job and flourish, and would the white man slip to the bottom of the ladder and turn to larceny? This social experiment is engineered by two grand old farts of Wall St, Don Ameche and Ralph Bellamy (a master of the cuddly uncle with a hidden agenda; he was Sapirstein, the satanist quack in *Rosemary's Baby*) in the form of a one-dollar wager. Despite some chucklesome set-pieces and performances, especially from Dan Ackroyd who achieves a minor miracle in conjuring our sympathies for his detestably smug spoilt brat character, and Denholm Elliott, whose outwardly complaisant butler views the proceedings with the last remnants of English dignified reserve and a simmering hatred for the pettiness of the bourgeoisie, *Trading Places*' conclusion is a glum one. Beneath the skin, this film reports, blacks and whites are really all the same, namely avaricious, spiteful, vengeful and self-obsessed. Even more astonishing in its misanthropy is *The Magic Christian* (1969), an all-star melange of sketches wherein multi-zillionaire Sir Guy Grand (Peter Sellers) amuses himself by playing nasty practical jokes to test how low people will stoop for money. "You've really got to hate people to love this film," opined Spike Milligan, who played the traffic warden that scoffed down a violation ticket, for a fistful of fivers: "I loved every inch of it."

Meantime was made by Mike Leigh at the same time as *Trading Places*, and set in Bethnal Green, less than two miles away from London's Stock Exchange—but it could just as well be a galaxy away. *Meantime* revolves around the non-adventures of the Pollock family. The dad and the two sons are unemployed—in Colin(Tim Roth)'s case, unemployable; withdrawn and incompetent, he resembles a mongoloid Elvis Costello—and fritter their days gazing at the gogglebox in their cramped tower block flat or listlessly meandering the deserted streets, maybe stopping off at a dull pub for a flat pint. Mavis (Pam Ferris), the mum, is chained to the kitchen, set free only to join the other crazed housewives at the bingo hall for a desultory evening. A born loser, not even her pen works. Whilst she is at breaking point from frustration and boredom, the male Pollocks wear their lassitude heroically, if not happily. *Meantime* is a penetrating and perceptive study of how money (rather, the complete absence of it) keeps a family together and tears them apart. There is uncomfortable fun to be had in eldest son Mark (Phil Daniels) verbally sparring with his indolent dad, Frank (Jeff Robert):

FRANK: If you want money, get out and earn it.

MARK: What—like you?

FRANK: I've done my stint, mate, don't you worry.

MARK: What—on the never-never?

FRANK: What's that supposed to mean?

MARK: You don't own nothing!

FRANK: Course I do.

MARK: What?

FRANK: You're sitting on 'alf of it!

MARK: What—this chair?

FRANK: Yeahhhh.

MARK: How can one chair be half of a three-piece suite? [...] You don't own this chair, you don't own this flat, you don't own nothing.

(Defeated, Frank stares blankly at the TV.)

Mark enjoys only temporary cheer from his word-whipping because he knows he will be exactly like Frank in time. (They already look alike with their grubby little moustaches.) He realises he's in a killer cycle but he can't find a way out, so he taunts and piss-takes anyone and everyone within earshot because that's all he can do. It's his pressure valve. His slightly more upmarket Auntie Barbara and Uncle John have middle-class aspirations (John's planning a patio) but the white-collar life and the disposable income brings on a new set of anxieties. Barbara can't cope with the tedious predictability of the home-owning set, nor the fat, complacent bore her husband has become, and gets outside of a vodka bottle and trashes their precious property.

The Pollocks exist in paltry, diminished, hand-to-mouth circumstances like the withered, beaten grotesques in *Jabberwocky* but this time the Monster is not skulking in the woods. It's omnipresent, all-powerful and being nurtured and fed by its keepers at The Stock Exchange, The IMF, and on Wall Street.

ELEVEN YEARS, 35 BACK ISSUES

1: August '93
SOLD OUT
Dr Johnson
Terence McKenna

2: Nov~Dec '93
SOLD OUT
Homer Simpson
Will Self

3: Jan~Feb '94
£8.00
Bertrand Russell
Charles Handy

4: April~May '94
SOLD OUT
Kurt Cobain
Matt Black

5: July~Aug '94
SOLD OUT
Douglas Coupland
Jerome K Jerome

6: Sept~Oct '94
SOLD OUT
Easy Listening
Richard Linklater

7: Dec~Jan '95
SOLD OUT
Sleep
Gilbert Shelton

8: Feb~Mar '95
SOLD OUT
Jeffrey Bernard
Robert Newman

9: May~June '95
SOLD OUT
Suzanne Moore
Positive Drinking

10: July~Aug '95
SOLD OUT
Damien Hirst
Will Self

11: Sept~Oct '95
£4.00
Keith Allen
Dole Life

12: Nov~Dec '95
£4.00
Bruce Robinson
All Night Garages

TO ORDER YOUR BACK ISSUES:

Go to www.idler.co.uk, or call 020 7691 0320 with your credit card, or make a cheque out to "The Idler" and send it to: The Idler, Studio 20, 24-28A Hatton Wall, London EC1N 8JH. You must include P&P cost as follows:
P&P: **Issues 1-24: 50p per issue. Issues 25-34: £2 per issue. T-shirts £1 per item. For European Community, add 50%. For Rest of World, add 100%**

TO ORDER:
CALL:
020 7691 0320
OR VISIT:
www.idler.co.uk

13: Jan~Feb '96
SOLD OUT
Stan Lee
Life As A Kid

14: Mar~Apr '96
£4.00
Bruce Reynolds
Will Self

15: May~Jun '96
SOLD OUT
Hashish Killers
Alex Chilton

16: Aug~Sept '96
SOLD OUT
John Michel
World Poker

17: Nov~Dec '96
SOLD OUT
John Cooper Clarke
Cary Grant

18: Spring '97
SOLD OUT
Thomas Pynchon
Ivan Illich

19: Summer '97
£4.00
Psychogeography
Henry Miller

20: Winter '97
SOLD OUT
Howard Marks
Kenny Kramer

21: Feb~March '98
SOLD OUT
The Gambler
Bez

22: April~May '98
SOLD OUT
Alan Moore
Alex James

23: June~July '98
SOLD OUT
Summer Special
Tim Roth

24: Aug~Sep '98
SOLD OUT
Krazy Golf
David Soul

MAN'S RUIN 25: Winter 1999

£15

The first book-format Idler, featuring Louis Theroux's Sick Notes, Will Self, Howard Marks, Adam and Joe and Ken Kesey

PARADISE 26: Summer 2000

£5

Jonathan Coe meets David Nobbs, Nicholas Blincoe on Sherlock Holmes, Tiki Special, Iain Sinclair on the London Eye

THE FOOL 27: Winter 2000

£5

Village Idiots, World Of Pain, Arthur Smith's diary, The Big Quit, James Jarvis's World of Pain, John Lloyd

RETREAT 28: Summer 2001

£10

Louis Theroux meets Bill Oddie, Jonathan Ross meets Alan Moore, Alex James meets Patrick Moore, plus Andrew Loog Oldham

HELL 29: Winter 2001

£10

Crass founder Penny Rimbaud, Crap Jobs Special, Boredom Section, New fiction from Niall Griffiths, Mark Manning, Billy Childish

LOVE 30: Summer 2002

£10

Louis Theroux meets Colin Wilson, Johnny Ball on Descartes, Crap Towns, Devon Retreat, Chris Yates interview, Marchesa Casati

TO ORDER: CALL 020 7691 0320 OR GO TO WWW.IDLER.CO.UKNOW

THE VIEW FROM THE SOFA

Greg Rowland likes what he sees in the future

CHRIS WATSON

Money is the thing that you need to exchange for goods and services. The price of things is dependent on their exchange value, a relationship between supply/demand and cash in the economy and your personal pocket. You generate cash by creating or doing things that create a surplus value, the profit which capitalists accrue which makes them richer, providing more money for themselves and sometimes for employees, and certainly for the Government.

You might get cross about this process, if you feel overly exploited and alienated from it. If you're on the capitalist end then you're laughing. Maybe exchange values and capitalist surplus should be re-arranged more equitably in the future?

The revolution will happen one day. In the future, everyone will have whatever they want in material terms, and won't have to do much to get it. We're all familiar with how computers and IT stuff doubles in power and halves in price every eighteen months or so. If this process could be transferred to cars, house-building, aeroplanes and the production of energy then we'd be living in a very different world.

Of course here I am advancing a potential thesis in Experimental Marxism: What happens to Exchange Theory in an Age of the Replicator? In *Star Trek*, the replicator could furnish you with fine faux antiques, a cup of Earl Grey or, if you really wanted, a dozen gold Bentleys. As the advanced nanaite technology had infinite capabilities, based on an infinite energy source, getting any material possession, from a simple lead pencil to a gilded mansion would, in practical terms, involve a negligible differential in terms of labour and energy. Capital itself would be entirely missing from the equation. The question then arises of why anyone would want a gold Bentley, when its symbolism of exclusivity and individualism would be rendered meaningless by its potential for ubiquity. The Bentley would vanish into a logical void, similar to the kind of trans-dimensional void of unknowability that inhabits the staff of Dixon's when you ask them a simple question.

Therefore *Star Trek* technology, when it does happen, will be the true Marxist revolution—closer to the free-flowing exchange of pleasure and creativity imagined in Oscar Wilde's *Soul of Man under Socialism*. And best of all, the modes of production and consumption will be rendered entirely obsolete, leaving our descendents to sit about on sofas watching 300 years of old TV shows and be praised by the community at large for their serene indolence. Make it so....